Special Praise for *Loving Like You Mean It*

"Taking on nothing less than love, Dr. Ron Frederick swings and hits it out of the park with this must-read book. His clear, warm, and accessible style brings neuroscience, relationship theory, and years of clinical experience to help with our relationships. Reading this wise book you will not only understand why you do the things you do (even when you don't want to), but also how to change so that you can love and be loved."

Diana Fosha, PhD, Developer of Accelerated
Experiential Dynamic Psychotherapy and author of
The Transforming Power of Affect

o o o

"With compassionate understanding of the ways in which our early experiences shape our emotional lives, Dr. Ron Frederick offers an inspiring, practical guide to free yourself from the past and grow the capacity for stronger, happier relationships."

Elisha Goldstein, PhD, Co-founder of
The Center for Mindful Living in Los Angeles

o o o

"*Loving Like You Mean It* is a heartfelt, well written, and practical guide to applying mindfulness to the work of personal and relational transformation. Dr. Frederick brings you into his consulting room, sharing experiences from his work, and skillfully guides you down a path toward having more vital and rewarding relationships. Highly Recommended!"

Louis Cozolino, PhD, Psychology Professor at Pepperdine
University and author of *The Neuroscience of Human Relationships*

o o o

T0046942

LOVING

LIKE YOU

MEAN IT

Loving
LIKE YOU
MEAN IT

Use the Power of Emotional
Mindfulness to Rewire Your Brain
and Transform Your Relationships

RONALD J. FREDERICK

CENTRAL RECOVERY PRESS
LAS VEGAS

Central Recovery Press (CRP) is committed to publishing exceptional materials addressing addiction treatment, recovery, and behavioral healthcare topics.

For more information, visit www.centralrecoverypress.com.

Publisher: Central Recovery Press
              3321 N. Buffalo Drive
              Las Vegas, NV 89129

24 23 22 21   2 3 4 5

Library of Congress Cataloging-in-Publication Data

Names: Frederick, Ronald J., 1965- author.
Title: Loving like you mean it : use the power of emotional mindfulness to
   transform your relationships / Ronald J. Frederick, PhD.
Description: Las Vegas, NV : Central Recovery Press, [2019] | Includes
   bibliographical references.
Identifiers: LCCN 2018037678 (print) | LCCN 2018041956 (ebook) | ISBN
   9781942094951 (ebook) | ISBN 9781942094944 (pbk. : alk. paper)
Subjects: LCSH: Emotions. | Success--Psychological aspects.
Classification: LCC BF511 (ebook) | LCC BF511 .F74 2019 (print) | DDC
   152.4--dc23
LC record available at https://lccn.loc.gov/2018037678

Photo of Ronald J. Frederick by James DePietro.

Cover by The Book Designers. Interior design by Sara Streifel, Think Creative Design.

To my mother, for her unending love

and

To Tim, for opening the door to loving like I mean it

and wholeheartedly walking through it with me

TABLE OF CONTENTS

"In the end, only three things matter:

how much you loved,

how gently you lived,

and how gracefully you let go

of things not meant for you."

Buddha

INTRODUCTION

Since the beginning of time, in our hopes of fully enjoying love's rewards, human beings have struggled to understand its mysteries. By the time I was twenty, it had already become apparent to me that there was more to this thing called love than met the eye. I mean, the falling in love part—going from butterflies and sweaty palms to passion and euphoria in what seemed like an instant—was pretty easy and amazing. But it was the staying-there-and-making-it-work part that was already tripping me up. I just didn't get it. *Wasn't loving someone supposed to be fairly effortless*, I wondered? *Was there something I was missing or not getting? Was there something I was doing wrong?*

Not surprisingly, after a few failed attempts, but still hopeful I could crack the code, I landed in a psychotherapist's office. Thankfully, my therapist was a wise and caring older man sensitive to the human condition. A world traveler and lover of the arts, he had a penchant for sharing bits of poetry and literature with me in an effort to shed some light on my path. On one particular occasion, he shared something written by poet and novelist Rainer Maria Rilke:

> "For one human being to love another: that is
> perhaps the most difficult of all our tasks;
> the ultimate, the last test and proof, the work for
> which all other work is but preparation."

Those words struck a chord in me. Love, or loving well, is really hard. It takes work. Work that requires so much of us personally.

While it still wasn't clear to me just what kind of work I needed to do to be successful in love, Rilke's words helped me feel less alone. Not long after being introduced to that passage, I came across it on a greeting card, bought and framed it and hung it in my various homes over the years, a supportive reminder as I attempted to understand just what was required of me to love and feel loved.

Every day in my work as a psychologist I meet with people struggling to make love work. I hear about relationships that seem to start off well with such hope and promise but then go south. Those that are riddled with fighting, animosity, conflicts, or insecurity, and those that have become numbingly lifeless or distant over time. People describe feeling misunderstood, unappreciated, and put-upon. They struggle to understand how they could go from once feeling happy with their partners to now being awash in a sea of confusion, disconnection, hopelessness, and despair. Some can't identify anything particularly awful about their relationships but are troubled by a niggling sense that something's missing.

Many of them have worked incredibly hard to make their relationships better, do things differently, and get back on track. Some of them have even been in therapy before. But no matter how hard they've tried, they haven't been able to achieve any lasting success in their relationships. Invariably, they end up repeating the same patterns over and over again. Patterns that get them nowhere.

Sound familiar? If so, you're not alone. A recent study by the National Opinion Research Center at the University of Chicago found that relationship dissatisfaction is on the rise. More people are struggling to keep love alive than ever before.[1]

So, why do so many of us have a hard time?

Based on the people I encounter in my life both professionally and personally, my own life experience, and all the advances we've made in understanding how the human brain works, I've come to understand that, while our specific problems may differ, the underlying issue for most of us is the same. At the core of our struggles, festering beneath many layers of complaints is a fear of being emotionally present and authentic in our relationships. We are afraid of being ourselves.

Many of us are afraid to open up and step into our romantic relationships in a more honest and revealing way. Whether it's the ability to give or receive love, manage and express anger, sadness, or shame, or acknowledge the need for closeness and security, our capacity to be emotionally present with our partners is hijacked by fear—and it is fear that is keeping us from having the kinds of relationships we truly desire.

But why are we afraid of being emotionally present and authentic in our relationships?

The short answer is that our adult brains are still operating on wiring that was established in the first few years of our lives. Wiring that informs us how to be and, equally important, how *not* to be in the world. For many of us this wiring is outdated and not applicable to present-day living.

As the science of attachment has shown, early childhood experiences with our caregivers shape our emotional development and leave lasting imprints on the neural circuitry of our brains. When our caregivers are emotionally open and reliable, we develop the ability to balance and make good use of our emotions, calm and soothe ourselves, and emotionally relate to, and connect with, others. We develop a capacity to be emotionally present and engaged— essential components of healthy relationships.

However, when our caregivers react negatively to our emotional needs—for instance, become frustrated when we feel afraid and need their reassurance, withdraw when we feel hurt and need to be soothed, or admonish us when we're angry and assert ourselves—we learn to fear expressing ourselves. Instead of feeling emotionally safe to explore our relationships with our caregivers in a way that fosters learning and growth, we become anxious and hold certain feelings back, adjusting our behaviors to avoid the danger of disconnection from our loved ones.

In short, we suppress the feelings that threaten our sense of safety and security with our caregivers and amplify those that please them and thus allow us to maintain some degree of connection. Over time, our potential to manage and express our feelings is compromised, our emotional range becomes constricted, and the emergence and expression of our core self is thwarted, boxed in by the emotional parameters we had to adhere to as children.

To make matters more difficult, these powerful lessons about emotion and connection are stored in the parts of our memory that are outside of our awareness. That is, they operate on an unconscious level and guide our behavior *without us even knowing it*. Left unchallenged, they persist into adulthood and directly affect the ways we respond to our feelings, how we perceive and interact with our partners, and what we reveal or conceal of ourselves. Instead of having a flexible repertoire of relationship skills, many of us enter into the world of adult relationships emotionally ill-equipped and conditioned to react in ways that might have been useful at one time but now thwart real connection.

Consequently, when certain feelings or needs arise in our present-day relationships, we react defensively as though we're in real danger. We do everything we can to achieve some sense of safety. We develop patterns of being in the world that cover up what we truly feel inside. For example, instead of openly sharing how we feel or asking for what we need, we blame, criticize, or get demanding with our partners—or, conversely, we shut down, detach, and act as if we don't care when deep down underneath the layers of our defenses we really do care. We turn our partners into our latest remodeling project, or we try to mold ourselves into something seemingly more acceptable. Anything to feel internally and externally safe in the world.

While our childhood threat of danger no longer exists, many of us unknowingly continue to respond to our emotions, relationship needs, and desires as if they're dangerous. We end up repeating the same defensive patterns over and over—patterns that get us nowhere—as if we had no other options. In order to protect ourselves, we get caught in circular arguments with our partners, instead of taking the risk to share our hurt or fear. We minimize, deny, or hide our anger, pull away from our partners and avoid being direct, and then end up feeling resentful, disinterested, or depressed. Or, we fail to express the fullness of the love in our hearts—and then can't understand why our partners complain about feeling frustrated, alone, and unsure of our love.

Instead of *loving like we really mean it*, we move ahead on autopilot, at the mercy of our old brain wiring. Without a clue, we wonder why we're having such a hard time, why our relationships aren't more satisfying, and why we don't feel more connected. We ask ourselves, *"Is this as good as it gets?"*

Only when we recognize and attend to what's going on inside of us and find the courage to open up and be fully present with ourselves and in our relationships, only then can this picture really change.

Been There, Done That

I say this to you from a very personal place. My nervous system was shaped by my early experiences with my parents, both of whom had a fair amount of conflict and anxiety around emotion and connection. Despite their best efforts and love for me, neither was well equipped to help me or my sisters to develop the best internal road maps for navigating emotional connections. My early adult relationships were certainly a testament to this less-than-ideal conditioning.

While my relationships would start off well, within a matter of months they'd become challenging in all-too-familiar ways. They'd go from a sense of playfulness and willing discovery to a place where I found it harder and harder to get emotionally in sync and feel as though my partner and I were on the same emotional page. Our interactions were often fraught with tension, and conflict always seemed to be right around the corner.

I found it difficult to hear and trust my true feelings. Frequently I felt insecure and unsure. For instance, I'd feel angry or disappointed inside about something that happened between us but would then doubt myself, talk myself out of it, and avoid addressing the matter directly, not realizing that the feelings continued to live on somewhere inside of me, coloring my experience. Shared happiness was fleeting and not deeply felt, quickly short-circuited by a fear in me of what might happen next, such as that I'd say or do something wrong and mess things up. Although I longed for a sense of closeness and connection, when time alone together with a partner came, I felt restless and found it difficult to be still, to arrive, to be fully present.

I didn't realize how anxious I was under the surface—how much fear was pulling the strings and affecting every move I made. Instead I racked my brain to figure out why it was so challenging. I read a ton of articles and books on relationships and diligently tried to follow their suggestions. I talked about it ad infinitum in years of psychotherapy. I even wrote my doctoral dissertation on "fear of intimacy" in relationships! Yet, no matter how hard I tried to understand and do things differently, I'd continue to slam into the same walls.

I'm not sure how much longer I might have gone on this way, but thankfully my journey brought me to the office of a psychotherapist who worked quite differently from what I'd previously experienced in therapy. Instead of trying to figure out what was going on in my head, we focused on what was going on emotionally inside of me. To my surprise I discovered just how difficult it was for me to be present with my feelings, especially with someone else.

While my previous work in therapy helped to illuminate some of the ways in which I'd been impacted by my attachment experiences with my parents, I began to see how the repercussions of that early learning was showing up in the here and now, activating my nervous system, pushing me and pulling me in different directions, and causing me to react defensively. On a deep, unconscious level I still expected that something bad would happen if I really opened up and expressed myself. The old software in my brain kept giving off warning signals, reining me in, and forcing me down a narrow, well-worn path. If I was going to get anywhere different, anywhere better, I had to find a way to not get swept up in all the old, involuntary ways of responding. I needed to slow down, stay present, and deal with my discomfort, and find a different way forward.

It was challenging at first and scary, but over time space inside me opened up in which I could step back and observe what was going on and recognize when my old wiring was getting triggered. Instead of running or spinning around in my head, I learned to lean into and stay with my emotional experience. Gradually the grip of anxiety eased up, and I began to disentangle myself from my nervous system's old reactions.

With the buzz of my anxiety turned down, I was more able to connect with my core self—the self that knew how I felt, what I needed, and what I longed for. The self that wanted to reach out, connect, and be close. The self that my early conditioning had kept in check and covered up. Over time I found the courage to open up and express my truth and try new ways of relating and connecting with others, ways that felt more aligned with who I really am and how I wanted to be.

I see now that this was the work that I needed to be doing— the work that had eluded me for so long. I was learning a new and more authentic way of being with myself and with others. A way that would ultimately enable me to have the kind of relationship I truly desired. I no longer had to be a prisoner of my past.

Neither do you.

Something New

The main reason that our efforts to do things differently in our present-day relationships don't lead to lasting success is that, unbeknownst to us, the old wiring of our brain is running the show. No matter how hard we try to change our behavior, no matter how much we practice our listening, communication, or conflict resolution skills, if we're not aware of what's going on behind the scenes, sooner or later our nervous system gets activated, and we're up to our old tricks again, no longer in control. The bottom line is this: No real change in how we operate or interact can happen until we recognize and learn how to manage what's going on inside of us.

Fortunately in the last few years, great advances have been made in the field of neuroscience that have changed our understanding of how the brain works, develops, and changes. While we used to think that the hardwiring of our brain was set in stone by the time we reached adulthood, it's now well understood that the brain is "plastic," which means it remains malleable over a lifetime and reorganizes, or "rewires," itself in response to new experiences—a process that is known as "neuroplasticity."

What that means is that we can change the way our brains are wired.

You may be wondering how this is accomplished. Well, we can't keep doing the same thing over and over again, as that won't lead to change. That will only reinforce what we're doing already. We need to do something different, something new. We need to have the kinds of experiences that will grow our capacity to be emotionally present with ourselves and others—the kinds of experiences that will help us to develop what I call "emotional mindfulness."

Emotional mindfulness applies the basic principles of mindfulness, or moment-to-moment awareness, to our emotional experience. Simply put, it's about attending to, being present with, and making good use of our feelings—both with ourselves and with others. Practicing the skills of emotional mindfulness changes the way our brains operate. By focusing our attention in positive and constructive ways, we can free ourselves from old habits and fears, befriend our emotional experience, and develop new ways of relating. Rather than suppressing or acting out, we can find a balanced way of being with our experience in which we can abide and work with what's inside of us and engage with our partners in healthier, more meaningful ways.

Cultivating the skills of emotional mindfulness isn't just a good idea—it's now empirically proven to alleviate distress, optimize functioning, and improve our overall mental health. Following the publication of my previous book in 2009, *Living Like You Mean It: Use the Wisdom and Power of Your Emotions to Get the Life You Really Want*, the emotional mindfulness-based, self-help approach that I introduced there and draw from in this book was used as the basis for research conducted through Linköping University in Sweden. Several studies in which participants read about and practiced tools to develop emotional mindfulness found it to be an effective treatment for anxiety, depression, and social anxiety.[2] Pretty cool, huh?

In addition, the benefits to our relationships are numerous. In fact, as renowned relationship expert John Gottman suggests, the better a couple is at understanding, honoring, and working with their feelings, the more likely it is that their relationship will be successful and endure.[3]

When we're able to navigate our emotional experience mindfully and express our feelings, needs, and desires in ways that inspire our partners to do the same, it draws us together, increases our sense of safety, security, and trust, and strengthens our connection. On more solid footing, we're better able to manage conflict, repair rifts, and get back on track. Emotional presence infuses our relationships with energy and vitality. It also increases our sexual desire. Empathy and compassion grow between us, and we learn to support each other emotionally more freely. When we're able to understand and share our innermost feelings, we're better able to get the kind of caring we need from our partners, and, in turn, our partners feel important, valued, and loved. Overall, our relationships are imbued with a deep and abiding intimacy and, as such, are more gratifying and lasting.

Being present with and sharing our feelings, needs, and desires with our partners has the power to transform both our minds and our relationships. That is, if we can find the courage to get out of our comfort zone and be present and engage with our partners in a more open and vulnerable way. The challenge we face is in breaking free from the old wiring in our brains that is keeping us from these riches.

An Inside Job

Of course, as the saying goes, "it takes two to tango." Our partners are responsible for themselves and the role they play, and we need to collaborate and learn how best to work with each other. But the self that we bring to the dance of love is a crucial factor in our relationship success. Are we showing up with limited emotional and relational skills? Or are we flexible and agile, able to navigate and respond to the music of our emotions? Are we bringing our best self to our relationships or one that is compromised?

While who we are and how we manage our feelings is not our fault—after all, our brains are the product of not only our early environment but also millions of years of evolution and our genetic inheritance—given the choices that neuroplasticity affords us, isn't it our responsibility to become better stewards of our emotional selves?[4] In order to give our relationships a fighting chance, we need to. As psychologist and co-developer of mindful self-compassion, Christopher Germer, explains, "Transforming relationships with others starts with us; it's an inside job."[5]

Besides, does it feel fair or acceptable to you to have to sacrifice your happiness to the wiring of your childhood? Never being able to realize your full potential? Never being able to go the distance in your relationships? Somewhere inside of you, behind the anxiety, fear, guilt, or shame, is your core self—the self that knows your truth, how you feel, what you need, and what you want. The self that can feel and express a full range of feelings is able to see things clearly and responds accordingly. Your most resourced self who can deal openly and effectively when times are hard. Your compassionate, loving self who can be open, close, and connected. The self you were meant to be were it not for some less than ideal early programming. Isn't that the person you want to bring to your relationship? Take a moment or two and ponder this question. What do you imagine your life might be like if you did?

Change can begin with just one of us when we do our part to help shift the relational dynamics in a positive direction. We can come to our relationships better equipped to navigate our emotional experiences and give them our all. Personally, I can attest to how much better things go in my marriage of over twenty years when I slow down and attend to what's going on inside of me *and* do the work to communicate in a mindful way.

When we mindfully share our core feelings, we give our partners the opportunity to know us more deeply and to respond in new and different ways. We maximize our relationship's potential to be a place of growth and healing. If we really want our lives to change, if we really want to feel close to our partners, and them to us, we have to find the courage to share our deepest selves—the sadness we feel when hurt, the anger we feel when wronged, the vulnerability we feel when insecure, the love we feel when we care deeply, and the happiness we feel when we're loved in return.

Now, I'm fully aware that it's hard to try something new. Venturing out of our comfort zone can be anxiety provoking. When I started to be more open, and hence more fully present in my relationship, it was quite a scary prospect for me. I wasn't really sure how it would go and at times it filled me with fear. But it got easier. And it's not like I jumped in hook, line, and sinker. It was more of a one step at a time approach. Developing emotional mindfulness works the same way—it's not an all or nothing proposition. It's a process that, with repeated practice, strengthens over time. So, if you're feeling a bit daunted by the prospect of doing this, that's very normal. But not to worry, as there's a way of going about it that can make facing our fears more manageable.

The solution lies in finding a way to reduce your internal distress enough so that you can get some distance from your embedded patterns of behavior and begin to give both being with your feelings and expressing them a chance.

And, last but not least, you don't have to do it alone. I'm going to help you.

About This Book

For over twenty years, I have practiced and taught an attachment-based, emotion-focused model of psychotherapy developed by psychologist Diana Fosha called Accelerated Experiential Dynamic Psychotherapy (AEDP).[6] Hardly a day goes by in which I'm not deeply moved by the power of AEDP to help people break through the barriers that have constrained them and experience a deeper level of emotional intimacy in their lives. I'm writing this book because I want the same for you. I want to help you free yourself from old constraints so that you can bring your best self to your relationships, and have the relationships that you really want.

Drawing from my practice of AEDP, I'm going to share with you what I teach my clients every day: a proven four-step approach to overcome fear and connect more deeply with yourself and others. While our focus will be on helping you improve the quality and experience of your romantic relationships, this approach can also be used to help you better navigate and improve all kinds of relationships with people you love—whether they be friends, children, or family members.

This book is divided into three sections: Part One helps you better understand why and how your past is showing up in your present; Part Two provides the skills you can develop to help manage your emotional experience, separate your core self from your old wiring, and engage with your partner in a healthy, productive way. You'll learn how you can apply those skills in your life and bring your best self to your romantic relationships; Part Three illustrates what the four steps look like in action.

Having a better understanding of yourself, your behavior, and how your brain operates, can enable you to approach the work of change from a more effective and caring place inside yourself. In Part One, "How We're Wired," we'll start our journey together by taking time to consider some important lessons from attachment theory and neuroscience that help to explain how early relational experiences shape our brains and lay down neural roadmaps that implicitly color our perception and guide our behavior in relationships. We'll examine the emotional environment in which you spent your formative years and the subsequent styles of relating we tend to develop as a way of maintaining some sense of connection and safety with our caregivers. You'll become familiar with patterns of responding we typically get caught up in so that you can see more clearly how your early programming is getting played out in your current life and make better sense of your behavior.

+

In Part Two, "Updating Our Wiring," I'll teach you a four-step approach to developing and utilizing the skills of emotional mindfulness. With Step One, "Recognize and Name," you'll learn to identify when old programming has activated your nervous system's threat response, when you've been "triggered," so you can begin to break the pattern of habitual responding. In Step Two, "Stop, Drop and Stay," you'll learn to pause and make room, turn your attention inward, and abide with what's happening inside of you without being reactive. You'll learn strategies to ease your discomfort, attend to your inner wounds, and comfortably move through your feelings to a calmer and clearer place. No longer caught in the grip of fear, you can "Pause and Reflect," which is Step Three. This step is about gaining access to the wisdom that comes with being in touch with your core self, consider a now-broader range of options, and choose a course of action that is more aligned with your intentions and values. Lastly, in Step Four, "Mindfully Relate," you'll learn how to manage the anxiety that comes with opening up in a new and different way, stay centered and present, and express your truth in a manner that will maximize the likelihood of you being heard and received. All of the chapters in this section include a variety of simple tools and exercises designed to help you develop and strengthen a new way of being with yourself and others. As with any skill, the more you practice, the better you get.

In addition, we'll explore the ways in which you can use the skills of emotional mindfulness to turn your relationship around and get back on track. For instance, you'll learn how to maintain emotional balance when engaging with your partner, especially when the going gets tough, so that you can see yourself more objectively and respond more effectively. I'll teach you how to recognize and get beyond your partner's defenses so you can avoid getting caught in old dynamics, open to a broader range of options, and explore healthier ways of relating. You'll also learn how to receive the good stuff that comes your way more fully—gratitude, encouragement, and love—and how to make better use of your innate capacity for empathy and compassion to deepen your connection.

In Part Three, "Rewiring in Action," we'll visit with three people, each with a different attachment style, and take a look at how they worked the steps in their lives.

Throughout this book, I'm going to share with you stories of people like yourself. People who felt frustrated, alone, and in despair, but who in facing their fears and taking the risk to be emotionally present with their partners, saw their relationships change in ways they hadn't imagined possible. My hope is that you might recognize yourself in some of these stories and feel less alone—that you'll realize that the same can happen for you and be inspired to give it a try.

Mostly, what I want you to know is that with the right tools and regular practice, real change can happen. The capacity for healthy, loving connections is inside all of us, just waiting to come out. Are you ready to find a way to set it free and let it shine?

Come with me. Let's do it together. You'll see. Your relationship can be fuller and richer than you ever imagined. You can have the relationship you really desire and are meant to have. You can love like you mean it.

PART I:

HOW WE'RE WIRED

CHAPTER ONE

Making Sense of How You're Wired

"Memory believes before knowing remembers."
WILLIAM FAULKNER, *Light in August*

"This is going to sound strange," Nora began as her eyes widened, "but there's something about me saying 'thank you' to my husband that feels scary."

Nora, a client of mine in her early thirties, had been telling me about how her husband, Cliff, had accompanied her to a doctor's appointment the previous day. It was an anxiety-filled moment for her; she was getting the results of a mammography for a lump in her breast she'd found recently. In an uncharacteristic show of support, her husband had offered to go with her to the appointment. He sat beside her as they listened to the doctor give the test results. To their shared relief, she received a clean bill of health.

As they left the appointment, Nora felt the tension that had filled her body for the last few days begin to dissolve and make way for an upwelling of gratitude. She was grateful for her health and especially for her husband's care and concern, given all the marital strife that had been the stuff of her life for so long. They'd been working so hard to shift out of the negative patterns they'd been caught up in, and things between them finally seemed to be improving.

Nora wanted to thank Cliff to let him know just how much it meant to her that he'd been there for her when she really needed him. She recalled how I'd recently encouraged her to let her husband know how much she appreciated the efforts he was making to better their relationship and respond to her needs. Nora felt a "thank you" roll around the tip of her tongue, readying itself to be expressed, but her lips wouldn't separate. She couldn't get the words out. As she later described the feeling to me, she said it was as though a force field had enveloped her, freezing her body with fear and preventing any appreciation from being communicated openly.

Nora's eyes filled with tears as she recounted what had happened. "It doesn't make sense," she said, looking at me bewildered and shaking her head. "Why couldn't I just say thank you?"

It was a good question. Why would uttering a simple "thank you" to her husband feel dangerous to Nora? I knew that the answer wasn't something we could reliably get to by merely thinking about it. To get to the heart of the matter, we needed to consult the wisdom of Nora's body.

"Well, it may not make sense on a rational level," I explained, "but clearly something about expressing gratitude to Cliff really scares you. That's what we need to pay attention to. Your body seems to know more about what's going on than your head."

"Let's try something," I suggested. "Close your eyes, and picture that moment with Cliff. Imagine trying to thank him and just notice what happens inside of you. What do you feel?" Nora closed her eyes and recalled that moment. Within seconds she was in touch with something; her eyes opened quickly and widened with fear. "What's coming up for you?" I asked.

"My chest feels tight, and my heart is racing. It's that same panicky feeling I get sometimes."

"What's so scary?" I wondered aloud empathically and then pointed her toward the answer. "Ask the fear, not your head."

"It feels like something bad is going to happen," Nora replied. "I don't know . . . like I'm going to be rejected."

○   ○   ○

What's Actually Going On

What's going on with Nora? What's making her feel so afraid? She's been longing for her husband to be more present and engaged, and to put her and their relationship first. You'd think the gratitude she's feeling would just flow right out of her. Instead, when the opportunity presents itself, why does expressing her feelings frighten Nora? Why is she afraid to be emotionally open and to connect more deeply with her husband?

For that matter, how is it that so many of us become this way—afraid of being emotionally open in our relationships?

This is certainly not how we start out in life. Our ability to express ourselves openly and connect with others is apparent from the time we're born, and it expands by leaps and bounds during the first few years of life. Over the last few years, I've had a front row seat to this developmental phenomenon while spending time with my adorable nephew Ethan. Apart from being totally enamored with him (which, I confess, I am), I'm repeatedly struck by how readily and vividly he experiences and communicates his emotions. He smiles and laughs with delight when he's happy, cries when he's sad, and gets angry when frustrated in some way. His face lights up with love and affection when he sees his parents, and he reaches out for contact and reassurance when he's afraid. It's amazing to witness the simplicity and clarity of his feelings and his natural capacity to communicate and connect emotionally.

This emotionally expressive child wonder provides such a stark contrast to Nora and to so many adults whom I encounter both professionally and personally. Of course, the manner in which we express our feelings becomes more sophisticated as we grow and mature. With the right kind of help, we learn how to manage our feelings and communicate our experience verbally. But if we're born emotionally uninhibited, what happens to us? How do we become so afraid of sharing our feelings with others? How do we lose this ability to be in touch with our feelings and connect emotionally?

The answer can be found by looking at our earliest relationships.

Wired to Connect

Attachment theory, one of the most empirically supported perspectives on human development and relationships, explains how our early emotional experiences with our parents shape who we are, how we see the world, and how we behave in relationships. Initially proposed by renowned British psychiatrist John Bowlby, it is based on the assertion that as human beings our need to be in a close relationship with someone is fundamental to our existence.[1] It starts from the time we're born and continues throughout our lives. Our primary instinct, wired in by millions of years of evolution, is to seek contact, comfort, and connection.

At no point in our lives is this more apparent than when we are just born. As infants, we come into the world completely helpless, entirely reliant on our parents to take care of us, to bathe, clothe, and feed us, to soothe our fear and distress, and to protect us from harm. In addition, our social and emotional development is dependent on our parents being attuned, responsive, and engaged with us. Unlike other mammals, it takes years of nurturing support before we humans are able to make a go of life on our own.

Our caregivers are of utmost importance to us. They provide our lifeline. It's no wonder then that we are biologically programmed to develop and build a connection with them. If we didn't, we wouldn't survive. Literally.

It follows that maintaining a secure attachment with our caregivers is a high-stakes matter, and the drive to do so overrides all of our other primary needs. In short, we do whatever it takes to stay connected to them in order to prevent the possibility of loss or abandonment, which is the equivalent of death to an infant or child.

Our infant "M.O.," so to speak, is all about maintaining a secure connection with our primary caregivers at all costs.

One way we experience that connection is through actual physical closeness. For instance, when our parents hold us or take our hand, or when we reach out and make physical contact. This is particularly true when we are infants, and physical contact is a primary source of connection. However, the main way we experience a connection with our caregivers and how it gets wired in is through emotion. We sense and experience connection and disconnection through our feelings and the emotional responses they engender as well as through the feelings of others.

As babies, we don't have words to express what's going on with us. Instead everything is communicated through feelings, and feelings are expressed nonverbally—through the "language" of the face, the eyes, and the body, and through touch, sounds, vocal tones, and rhythms. We let others know about our experience by expressing our feelings physically, and in return we learn about others by sensing and reading their feelings.

In the best of circumstances, our caregivers are emotionally available and respond to our communications in an attuned way, delighting in our joy, soothing our fears, and lovingly meeting our needs for closeness and care. When we express ourselves and experience a sense of engagement and understanding from our caregivers, we feel seen, heard, and validated. When we are emotionally in sync, we feel close, connected, and on secure ground. We feel safe. In this way, attachment and emotion are inextricably linked—connections are formed and maintained through emotional experiences.

Now, I'm not suggesting that our parents had to be perfect all the time and meet our every emotional expression with one hundred percent empathic attunement. That's just not humanly possible. Of course, there were moments when they were distracted, anxious, or irritated, or when their initial response was less than ideal. But if our caregivers are able to recognize what happened, reengage, and repair the disconnection, then together we get back on track and continue onward with our relationship and ourselves intact.

In fact, studies have shown that when our caregivers are able to navigate emotional ruptures with us, it actually strengthens our connection to them and makes us feel more secure in the world. We come to learn that our relationship can weather disruptions. The road may get rocky at times, but our bond will endure. This lesson is of utmost importance. Knowing that we'll find our way even if things go awry helps build our sense of internal security. After all, if you're assured that the relationship will go back to normal after the storm has passed, there's good reason not to worry too much about it.

Countless repetitions of optimal back-and-forth emotional exchanges with our parents, in which feelings are expressed, registered, and responded to, not only help us feel connected and secure in our connection but also provide the experiences through which we learn how to understand and make good use of our emotions. In fact, our emotional development directly reflects our parents' capacity to help us cope with and manage our feelings, especially when those feelings are intense or overwhelming, which is often the case in infancy and childhood.

When our parents help us regulate our emotions—that is to calm the intensity, stay present, and work through the experience— we eventually develop the ability to deal with our feelings ourselves in a healthy way. We develop an internal capacity to regulate and make good use of our emotions. The broader the range of feelings we learn to manage when we're children, the larger and more flexible our emotional range will become as we grow and develop. Having that flexibility is a very good thing: As studies in emotional intelligence show, knowing how to manage and make good use of our feelings paves the way for success in life and in our future relationships.[2]

Unfortunately, many of us grow up with parents who are uncomfortable with some or all emotions—both their own and those of others.

That's when things go awry.

As babies we're extremely sensitive to the emotional cues we receive from our caregivers: what we see in their faces, their eyes, what we sense in their bodies. When our parents are uncomfortable with certain feelings and react negatively to them, even subtly, we pick up on this. For instance, when our anger offends them and they admonish us, or when our fear irritates them and they get impatient or annoyed. Another example is when our need for closeness overwhelms them and they withdraw. When we sense any sort of discomfort on the part of our caregivers, we get scared. Our caregivers' discomfort signals a threat of abandonment to our exquisitely perceptive nervous system. Thus, we keenly sense and learn from our earliest experiences which feelings and behaviors are acceptable to our parents and which ones aren't. We recognize which feelings make our parents uncomfortable and which ones bring them pleasure. And, more importantly, we become experts at which feelings draw and keep our parents close and which ones upset them or cause them to pull away.

Motivated by our innate drive to stay connected and the distress we experience when we're emotionally disconnected, we adjust our emotional repertoire accordingly. We either suppress the feelings that threaten connection, or we heighten those that keep our caregivers engaged. In short, we do whatever it takes to keep Mommy and/or Daddy close.

Isolated or occasional negative responses from our caregivers don't tend to have long-lasting effects, especially if the parents repair the disruption with attunement and connection and reengage in a more helpful way. But repeated patterns of unfavorable responses can cause children to exclude or distort the feelings that seem likely to cause a negative reaction from their caregivers and maybe even exaggerate those that seem to assure a sense of connection.

Suppressing or heightening certain feelings as children is quite adaptive since those responses help us stay connected to our parents and thus maximize the caretaking and connection we get. But these survival strategies come at a high cost: They compromise our inborn ability to feel, communicate, and share our core feelings. Over time, our development is thwarted, and our emotional and interpersonal capacity is diminished. We end up cut off from a fuller experience of ourselves and of our relationships.

○   ○   ○

Nora's Early Emotional Experience

Beneath Nora's fear of expressing gratitude toward her husband was a well of feelings. Love, vulnerability, sadness, and longing for closeness and connection to name just a few. These were feelings she had long ago learned to suppress and conceal; they were too dangerous to have when she was growing up. Early on in our work together, as I helped Nora turn down the dial on her anxiety and make room for the feelings inside her, a picture of her early life emerged that began to shed light on the origins of her current struggle.

Nora was born into an unsettling and unstable environment. Her mother, barely twenty, and her father, thirty-five, were not married and had a rocky relationship. While Nora's father was seldom around, when he was his attention was consumed by Nora's mother. Nora longed for her father's attention. To be seen, cared for, and loved by him. But he was frequently distracted and seemed to have little patience. Occasionally pleasant toward one another, her parents spent most of their limited time together arguing. Nora was also shocked to learn later that her father had a family with another woman in town and spent most of his time with them.

After many failed attempts at trying to make their relationship work, Nora's parents decided to go their separate ways when she was six. The memory of their painful goodbye haunted Nora as she grew into adulthood, the moment vividly etched in her memory and never too far from her awareness. She could still see herself and her mother boarding the train, which would take them to her grandmother's house, while her father remained outside on the station platform. Feeling heartbroken and abandoned, Nora stared at her father through the window of the train as it pulled away, his sullen face growing smaller and smaller until it disappeared in the distance. She sat motionless in her seat, filled with unbearable sadness. Inside her, a growing sense that there must be something wrong with her, that she must be unlovable and unworthy began to take root. After all, Nora's six-year-old mind reasoned, why else would he let her go? Nora never saw her father again.

Nora's mother, the one constant in her early life, was anxious and unpredictable. In many ways, she was still a girl herself, preoccupied with her own concerns and developmentally unready for the job of parenting.

Because she was a fearful person, Nora's mother could be overprotective, gravely warning Nora of the dangers of the world and giving her explicit instructions on how she should protect herself from harm. But rather than feel safe and protected, her mother's cautionary tales only exacerbated in Nora a looming sense of danger that something bad would happen.

While she could be loving at times, her mother was usually distracted and oblivious to Nora's emotional needs and attempts to gain her attention. When she did notice, she often seemed irritated and would react in a dismissive way, sometimes criticizing Nora for being silly or unreasonable. On one particular occasion, Nora recalled leaning over to kiss her mother's arm after her mother had bumped it against something and seemed to have hurt herself. Her mother, unable to control her distress and receive her daughter's affection, lashed out. "Don't touch me!" she blurted out as she pulled away, leaving Nora feeling confused, hurt, and ashamed.

Perhaps trying to make up for when she'd been neglectful or reacted badly, Nora's mother would also occasionally swoop in out of nowhere with a dramatic show of affection. While you might think this change in behavior would be a welcome occurrence for Nora, more often than not, it felt excessive and smothering—more about her mother's needs and less about her own. It didn't give Nora the kind of sensitive and attuned love and care that she needed.

Never quite sure what to expect and fearful of possibly being shamed or rejected, Nora learned to avoid explicitly communicating her needs for closeness and care and to inhibit any show of affection. However, her innate need for connection was too strong to contain and found its way out in the form of behavioral ticks and inexplicable ailments. Not realizing her daughter's behavior had an emotional basis, her mother would take her to the doctor, trying to get it to stop or get some medicine to make the symptoms go away. It was the one thing that would reliably get Nora's mother to engage with her.

As a child, Nora learned what would bring her mother close and what would drive her away. In a fundamental way, Nora learned to dismiss her own emotional needs and stuff down any feelings that might make her mother uncomfortable, engender her disdain, or set her off. Nora did what she needed to do to keep her mother happy and to feel a sense of connection with her. Underneath it all, she was suffering, longing to be cared for, comforted, and embraced in a whole and unconditional way. Her natural affection had nowhere to go. It was a valid way for a child to cope with an untenable situation, and it helped Nora get through her early years with her family as best as she could.

Over time this pattern of pleasing others and neglecting her own feelings became her standard way of responding and, therefore, left Nora disconnected from her emotional experience as well as from those she was closest to, including her husband. The pattern that had helped her maintain a connection with her mother as a child had now become a liability.

As I helped Nora become more emotionally mindful of what was going on inside of her, she began to see how hard it was for her to be vulnerable with her husband, to let her more loving feelings show, and how, in a way, she'd become imprisoned by her fear of being rejected or dismissed. Underneath it all, she longed to be cared for and embraced in a whole and unconditional way, and, as she put it, "be the person that I really am."

Outdated Wiring

You might be wondering why Nora's fear would persist. After all, she's a grown woman now and doesn't have to worry about her mother's reactions. Besides, even if her husband were to react badly to her showing her softer side (not likely, actually), she should be able and free to express how she feels regardless, shouldn't she? There's some truth to this line of thought. Nora is an adult, and she should feel safe and free to be her own person. The problem is that her brain is running on old programming and will continue to operate in this way until she's able to recognize what's going on with her and start to get some distance from her wired-in, preconditioned nervous system's responses.

To make sense of these physiological dynamics in all of us, it helps to have a bit of an understanding about how the brain develops and works.

The human brain is a "social organ." It thrives when it has stimulating, interactive experiences with other human brains. In fact, our infant brain, which is relatively unformed when we're born, *requires* this emotional engagement with others in order for it to develop and mature. While genes determine the specific neuronal makeup of each brain, our experiences determine which neurons get activated. Without interpersonal brain-to-brain experiences, many of the neurons in our immature brains would wither and die. Connecting and relating with others in our environment gets our brain cells firing and wiring together to form the vast and person-specific neural circuitry of our brain—the programming, so to speak, that oversees how we operate.

The first few years of life form a critical period during which the brain is growing at a remarkable rate. The right hemisphere, the side of the brain that specializes in the nonverbal, expression, reception, and regulation of emotion, is the first to develop.

Our early life is spent in the world of the right brain: feelings, images, bodily sensations. The left hemisphere, which specializes in language and logical thinking, starts to develop a bit later. Evidence of its development is seen when babies become more verbal. The upshot of this sequence is that, for a fair amount of time, our right brain is running the show. There's a whole lot of brain development happening during the time when our experiences are all about feelings—sensing, perceiving, experiencing, and expressing emotion. Furthermore, since most of our experiences are with our caregivers, our emotion-based interactions with them have a disproportionate impact on the very architecture of our brains.

Let's take a closer look at what exactly happens.

As infants, our needs are fairly basic. Life is all about survival. We come into the world exquisitely attuned to whether or not we're safe. In fact, the part of our brain that assesses the threat of danger and activates our "fight-flight-freeze" response, the amygdala, is up and running before we're even born. From the get-go, we can tell how secure our little world feels and are prepared to respond if the need arises. If we don't feel connected to our caregivers, if we sense that they are not emotionally available and responsive, we become anxious and distressed. Our amygdala sounds the alarm that our safety and well-being are in jeopardy, activates our nervous systems, and mobilizes us to take action. Through trial and error, responding emotionally in different ways, we figure out how we need to behave in order to keep our parents engaged as well as to gain a sense of security and feel safe. These emotional lessons of what works to maintain connection—and what doesn't—get wired into our neural circuitry.

When our parents respond to our emotions in an attuned, accepting, and encouraging way, we come to associate our feelings and their expression with a positive sense of connection, and we feel safe to share them. For instance, when a mother meets her child's sadness with empathy and concern, the child feels seen and cared for. Children learn that it is helpful to express their emotional pain, that it will bring them the comforting they need, that they will feel better, and that they can trust that someone will lovingly be there for them. My three-year-old nephew Ethan is fortunate in that he has very attuned, emotionally available caregivers; the result is that he is able to express himself so freely. In attachment terms, he would be seen as being "securely attached" to his caregivers.

If, on the other hand, the response to his emotional expressions were given in a way that raised his levels of anxiety, they would become linked in his memory with a sense of danger. For example, when a father gets frustrated or is irritated by his children's fear and vulnerability and responds with impatience or dismissiveness, they learn that showing these feelings as well as the need for reassurance and care are dangerous. Instead of feeling seen and understood, children who are responded to in less than optimal ways come to feel that certain aspects of their emotional selves are bad and harmful and need to go away.

This is what happened with Nora. Her mother responded negatively to her need for affection and closeness and, in turn, Nora learned to suppress it out of fear of rejection.

For better or worse, the more a particular interaction is repeated during childhood, the stronger these associations and the related neural pathways become. As the saying goes, "neurons that fire together, wire together."[3] Eventually, depending on our experiences, either safety or fear becomes embedded in our brain's circuitry as an automatic response to our feelings. These potent lessons about emotion and connection—about how relationships work and what we can anticipate—form instructional blueprints, or what Bowlby referred to as "internal working models," that get stored outside of our awareness in our long-term memory.[4] The effects of this hardwiring are powerful and long lasting.

Memory

There are two types of long-term memory, "explicit" and "implicit," and they differ in a very important way. Information stored in explicit memory requires conscious effort on our part to be recalled. When you're trying to remember what time you agreed to meet a friend for dinner or where you celebrated a particular birthday, you're making use of explicit memory. In contrast, information stored in implicit memory requires no conscious effort on our parts to recall. Implicit memories are what afford us the ability to do things like ride a bike, button a shirt, or type on a keyboard without having to think about it.

Our early lessons about emotion and relationships get organized into mental models—schemas, templates, or maps— that are stored in the implicit memory, the only form of memory available to us when we're infants. They contain a set of beliefs and expectations about our own and other's people's behavior, our self-worth, whether or not we're lovable, and whether we can depend on others to be there for us (see sidebar). These internal working models persist into and throughout our adult life, coloring and shaping our perceptions of our partners and ourselves and guiding our responses without us even knowing it. In short, they develop into the unconscious programming for how we do relationships and are especially dominant when strong emotions get aroused.

INTERNAL WORKING MODELS

• Implicitly stored schemas or templates
of how relationships work

• Are based on our early attachment
experiences with our caregivers

• Contain a set of beliefs about who we
are and what other people are like

• Tell us what to expect and what to
do when we relate with a partner

• Unconsciously color our perceptions
and guide our behaviors

It just so happens that the storehouse for these memories includes the part of our brain that assesses whether or not we're in danger—our amygdala. What we might call a "threat detector," the amygdala appraises our level of safety based on previous experiences.[5] It scans our current situation and then runs a search through lessons stored in our neural files, our implicit memories, to see if there's any cause for alarm. If it finds a match, even one that's remote, it prompts us to respond as we have learned to do in the past. All of this takes place behind the scenes, outside the realm of our conscious awareness.

While this process has evolutionary value—better to be safe than sorry, even if we might be wrong, right?—it also can be a problem. When implicit memories are activated, they don't come with a time stamp. We don't realize that the surge in our nervous system is based on lessons from our distant past and might not be entirely relevant to the situation in front of us. Instead, we interpret what we're feeling as a result of whatever is happening in the here and now and respond in the way we're programmed to respond. We keep reacting as though we're in danger, whereas, in reality, most of the times we're not.

This is precisely what's happening for Nora. She fears that she's going to be rejected if she expresses her gratitude, but she isn't.

○   ○   ○

Nora's Wiring

Although Nora's memory of her childhood gives us a pretty good idea of why she's afraid to be emotionally open and vulnerable with her husband, the groundwork for her fear was set in place in events that occurred even earlier than the ones she remembers.

To illustrate how this process unfolds, let's imagine what life might have been like for Nora when she was a baby. Given what we know about Nora's mother, it's reasonable to assume that the stress of having and caring for a tiny baby, mostly by herself, pushed her mother to her emotional limits. In addition, Nora's mother brought to this experience her own attachment history—her own implicit memory bank of how *her* mother responded to her when she was an infant, which, in turn, affected how she responded to her own daughter. When Nora cried or fussed, as babies inevitably do, her mother may have felt overwhelmed or inadequate, reacted with discomfort, or pulled away. Maybe she got frustrated or angry with her. Perhaps she felt ashamed about her own inadequacy and, as a result, was shaming.

From baby Nora's point of view, these responses implied the threat of abandonment (which would lead to death) and were terrifying. In response, her brain's threat system lit up right alongside the parts of her brain that were activated by her initial feelings and behaviors (e.g., sadness, crying, reaching out), and these experiences became linked. Her brain encoded these associations between certain emotions and her mother's fear-inducing responses into a neural network, which eventually got wired into her brain's circuitry.

In a very basic way, on a nonverbal level, Nora learned that expressing certain feelings was treacherous. *If I'm vulnerable, Mommy gets anxious. If I'm upset, Mommy gets angry.*

What was she to do to cope with such a challenging situation? Sensing these negative reactions and geared to do whatever she needed to do to survive, Nora adjusted her behavior accordingly to keep her mother connected, to keep her present, to minimize any discord, and to prevent being scolded. She did what she needed to do to stay connected and as safe as she could. In short, in order to survive she stopped herself from having certain feelings.

Seen through the lens of her early attachment experiences, Nora's current struggle makes more sense. Her fear is triggered by implicit memories of early experiences in which having and showing her feelings *was* a scary prospect. Even though present-day circumstances are different, Nora's brain still anticipates the same responses she experienced as a child. Her brain is wired in such a way that now, whenever she starts to feel certain feelings, her nervous system responds as though she's in danger. As a result, Nora often feels anxious and afraid regardless of whether or not it's warranted. That's why she couldn't bring herself to say "thank you" to her husband. It was just too scary to allow herself to be vulnerable in that way with him.

This is exactly what's going on for those of us who are afraid to express our feelings and needs to others. *The fear we have around being emotionally open and connected is an old fear based in the past, not in the present.* Even though the fear itself is very much experienced in the here and now, our response is really the result of early programming. We're still responding as though there's a reason to be afraid and, in most instances, there isn't.

Your Early Experience

While Nora was well aware of her fear in the present moment, she had no idea that her nervous system was being triggered by the past, and that's true for many of us. We don't realize that the reaction we're having today was wired in a long time ago. To begin to separate out the influence of the past on our nervous system from the reality of the experiences of our present, it helps us to get a picture of what our early attachment experiences were like.

While many of the foundational experiences that shaped the wiring of your brain occurred further back then you can remember, chances are, the ways in which your parents reacted to and dealt with your feelings early on had a similar flavor to how they continued to respond to you throughout your childhood. Those later memories are likely more accessible to you. So, let's take a moment to get a sense of the early emotional environment in which you spent your formative years and how your feelings were responded to by your parents as you were growing up. This was one of the first things that Nora and I did in our work together.

Take some time to consider these questions (separately for each parent):

- How did your parent(s) respond to your feelings?

- Were they generally open, attentive, and responsive to your feelings?

- Did they get uncomfortable or anxious when you expressed your feelings or certain feelings in particular (e.g., anger, sadness, fear, joy, and the like)?

- Did they get distracted or seem to ignore certain feelings?

- Were some feelings okay and others not? If so, which feelings were welcomed, and which weren't?

- Did they get irritated, frustrated, or maybe even angry at times when you expressed your feelings?

- Were they shaming or admonishing toward your feelings in any way?

- Did they seem to take your feelings personally? Did you end up feeling as though you had to take care of them?

- How did they respond when you were afraid or feeling vulnerable? Did they comfort you? Did they protect you?

- How did they respond when you were angry and asserted yourself?

- How did they respond when you were affectionate and loving?

- Did they apologize and make amends when they hurt your feelings or reacted in an unhelpful way?

- Were their responses consistent or erratic?

- Could you rely on them to be there for you emotionally when you needed them?

- Did you feel loved? Seen? Valued?

- Overall, did it feel safe for you to share your feelings with them?

My Early Wiring

As you look over your answers to these questions, take some time to think about the implications of the messages that were either explicitly or implicitly conveyed by each of your parents' behaviors. Are there messages that you unknowingly took to heart? Are they cemented into the beliefs that you have now? Do you see any similarities between your current behavior and what went on in your family? Let me give you an example from my own life of what I mean to convey through these questions.

I must have been around eight years old when I got caught up in some kind of heated, verbal struggle with my father. I don't remember what had happened, but I recall that he was yelling at me. Needless to say, my father didn't deal well with anger. In fact, it wasn't uncommon for him to explode at times in fits of rage. When that would happen, I was horrified.

Anyway, I'm not sure what I had done on this particular occasion that had gotten him so worked up, but I must have felt that he was being unfair in some way. I could feel the energy building up inside of me, and, as he turned his back on me to walk away, I blurted out, "I hate you!" Not an uncommon thing for a kid to say when feeling angry at his parents. What followed was, for me, the worst part. My father didn't say anything. Not then, and not for several days. He gave me the silent treatment. He ignored all of my attempts to get his attention or to try to reconnect with him. He acted as if I didn't exist. I felt alone, sad, guilty, and scared. As you can imagine, for a child of eight, it was an excruciating experience. It also wasn't the only time I got the silent treatment.

Obviously, my father wasn't a good role model for helping me to deal with anger constructively. Had he been, he might have asked me what was upsetting me so and would have helped me with my feelings. At the very least, he might have apologized for losing it and worked toward clearing things up between us. Instead, he responded in a way that was anxiety-provoking, guilt-inducing, painful, and the source of an indelible impression on me and my nervous system. In addition, the message here, conveyed through his behavior, was clear: Anger is bad and dangerous to a relationship; it brings disdain, loss of approval, and abandonment. That got wired in. It's no wonder that I grew to feel anxious about anger, worried that I might have upset someone or about what would happen if I felt angry and spoke up or asserted myself with someone important to me. These fears followed me into my adult. relationships where any sign of conflict with a partner, friend, or authority figure ignited the internal sense of dread in me that I might be rejected, that our relationship was in jeopardy.

Anytime I felt angry an old sense of danger would reverberate in my system, and I'd start to question myself, inevitably rationalizing away whatever was bothering me, and, in so doing, avoiding the discomfort that came with the prospect of honoring my anger and asserting myself. Unable to feel or trust my true feelings, I kept repeating the same old patterns that got me nowhere.

Taking Stock

It's not that my father didn't love me. I know now that he loved me very much.

However, he had a really hard time managing his emotions—the result of his own troubled early experiences in his family of origin. Surely something deep in his implicit memory had gotten triggered in that moment between us and had gotten the best of him, causing him to withdraw and shut down. A response that he wasn't able to control and had a difficult time finding his way out of. Without any insight into what was affecting him, he was actually doing the best he could at that time. Fortunately he's grown and changed a lot since then.

Fortunately so have I!

The case with your parents is probably the same—they did the best they could, given their own attachment experiences, the resultant issues, and how their brains were wired accordingly. What's important to keep in mind here is that taking stock of your early experience is not about placing blame. We're not trying to find someone to point a finger at. Rather, we're trying to gain insights into how we've been shaped by our early experiences so that we can better understand our present-day reactions and behavior patterns. In doing so, we can more readily identify and separate out what's old and archaic and can begin to make some room for something new.

Often, when people start to take stock of the effects of their upbringing, they begin to feel sad, angry, frustrated, or pained. It's natural that you may feel so as well. Honoring whatever feelings you have is also not about blaming your caregivers. It's about acknowledging and appreciating the truth of your early experience and how it has affected you. It's also part of the process of no longer being constrained by old messages, by old wiring. Give those feelings a lot of room so that they can be felt and processed through. It's an important step on the road to resolution and freedom.

O   O   O

Something New

As I worked with Nora in our session together to understand and manage her fear, she was able to trace it back to when it began. She saw herself as a little girl, alone in her room, missing her father, wondering why he had left, and wondering if her mother would ever be there for her in the way she hoped her to be. She saw more clearly how the fear she was feeling with her husband came from that old place. It wasn't safe for her as a child to be vulnerable, to allow others to be important to her, to have needs for closeness. She had to put those desires away. She understood now why the prospect of opening up, leaning forward, and showing her gratitude to her husband filled her with dread. She felt that letting him know she needs him, values him, and depends on him, put her at risk. At least, that's what her nervous system conveyed to her.

As the fear inside her started to settle, as she connected with her early experiences, she began to feel something inside her opening up. It was as though she could feel herself more solidly in the room with me, more as the adult she now was and less as the little girl. More her core self. "That's not who I am," she said. "I want to be able to express myself. I want to be close."

Later that day, at dinner with her husband, she thought about our work together. She wanted to try being the person she sensed she could be. She wanted to take a risk and express her gratitude, to let her husband know how she feels. As she leaned into the present moment, the old fear started to stir a bit, but this time Nora knew where it was coming from. She looked over at her husband, her heart beating a little faster, took a breath and said, "Um, I meant to say this before, but . . . I just wanted to thank you for going with me to my doctor's appointment. It meant a lot to me."

Her husband smiled, reached out, put his hand on hers, and said, "Anytime."

○   ○   ○

While there was more work for us to do together to help Nora more readily recognize and break free from the fears that had been governing her life, she'd taken an important step toward being able to identify and express her true feelings and connect with her husband in a more genuine and productive way. She was on her way toward having the kind of relationship she had always truly desired.

You're already on your way as well. By thinking about the early environment in which you were raised, you're beginning to shine the light of awareness and understanding on your own experiences.

Let's move on to Chapter Two and take a closer look at what's happening inside of you so that you, too, can start to disentangle yourself from outdated fears and free yourself to experience new possibilities.

CHAPTER TAKEAWAYS

- Our need to be in a close, secure relationship is innate and fundamental to our existence.

- Our brain is shaped by the early emotional exchanges and interactions we have with our caregivers.

- As infants, we're exquisitely attuned to emotional cues and whether or not we're safely connected to our caregivers.

- When our caregivers respond negatively to our emotions, those negative responses become linked in our memory with a sense of danger.

- As infants, we adjust our emotional repertoire by either suppressing the feelings that threaten our connection with our caregivers or by heightening those feelings that keep them engaged.

- Early lessons about emotion and connection are stored outside the realm of our awareness in implicit memory as working or mental models of how to function in relationships.

- Our brain continues to be malleable and open to growth, i.e., is plastic and can change over the course of our lives.

- New experiences in which we identify, manage, and constructively express our core feelings change the way our brains are wired.

CHAPTER TWO

You've Got to Have Style

"Not everything that is faced can be changed,
but nothing can be changed until it is faced."

JAMES BALDWIN

Karla looked at the clock on her desk. She hadn't heard from Emily, her partner, at all today. *That's weird*, she thought. Emily didn't seem quite herself that morning, and Karla figured that she must have not slept well. But, as the hours ticked by, she started to worry. *Is Emily upset with me?* she wondered, as a wave of anxiety started to build inside of her. *Did I do something to piss her off?* Karla traced back over the last few days in her mind to see if anything stood out. Nothing. *You're being silly*, she thought, and tried to focus back on her work. But the noise in her head wouldn't let up. *Maybe she's getting bored with me?* she thought, as the anxiety inside her ratcheted up and pervaded her afternoon. However, that night at dinner, while Emily regaled her with the events of her busy day, Karla didn't say anything about her feelings. Instead she sullenly stared at her food, secretly hoping that Emily would notice how upset she was, that Emily would reach out and make things better.

○   ○   ○

Craig sat down on the couch, opened his laptop, and put his feet up. It had been a long day at work followed by a casual evening out with his friends and Lydia, his fiancée, to celebrate her birthday. He was glad to finally be home, kick back, and relax. As he settled in and started to check his emails, Lydia, sat down next to him, put her arm on his shoulder, and said affectionately, "Hey there. What're you doing? I want some time with you." Craig instantly felt himself tense up inside. "What do you mean?" he asked, incredulous. "We've been together all this time?" "Yeah, but that was with your friends around," Lydia explained. "I want some alone time. Just us." Craig felt his shoulders tighten. *Why does she always do this?* he thought to himself. *She's so damn needy. No matter what I do, I just can't win.* "Can't I just get a minute to myself?" he said as he rolled his eyes, shut his computer, and walked into the other room in a huff.

○   ○   ○

Sheri sat on her bed shaking and sobbing. Things had started off so great with Rick, the guy she'd been seeing for the last few months, so great that she'd begun to think that maybe the loneliness and longing that had always plagued her was a thing of the past. *Maybe I'm not such a loser after all,* she thought. But when Rick started to talk about things that they might do together in the future, a familiar sense of distress grew inside her. Sheri tried to hide it, to seem happy and on the same page as Rick. But the more he leaned in, the more she was filled with a sense of dread. *He's going to see something in me he doesn't like, and I'll get dumped again. I just know it!* Unable to contain the storm inside her any longer, she exploded in a mess of feelings, accusing him of lying to her, and telling him to never call her again. Except now she was filled with regret. *What was I thinking? How am I going to live without him?* And then vowed to find a way to get him back.

○   ○   ○

While these three people are different in the ways in which they react, beneath the surface they all have something in common: They're all afraid to be emotionally open and present in their relationships.

- Karla's afraid to trust in Emily's love. No matter how much Emily has tried to reassure Karla, she worries that, at any moment, something will go wrong between them. Her fear gets the best of her and keeps her from dealing with her feelings in a direct and healthy way. Instead of finding the courage to express her disappointment or frustration and thus give Emily a chance to explain and possibly address her needs, she acts out her feelings by being distant and closed off, hoping that will get Emily's attention and draw her back in, hoping that her fear will go away, thus reducing her distress, if only for a moment. When Emily is actually there and engaged, Karly cannot take it in.

- Beneath his irritation, Craig is afraid to be open and close with Lydia. He's scared of being vulnerable, of having needs for connection and closeness, and of caring too deeply. Instead of honestly acknowledging his fears and working through them with Lydia, he pushes them down and bristles in the presence of her affection. Caught in a trap, he's unable to stay open and receive love, to respond in kind and express his love for her. He's unable to connect in a more meaningful way.

- Sheri longs to be close but fears it at the same time. She's so overwhelmed by her mixed feelings that she can't tell what's real versus what is only fear swirling around in her head. She can't sit with her feelings long enough to find her center, see what's actually going on, and try to show up to her relationship in a balanced way. Instead of coming clean with Rick about the struggles she feels and trying to deal with them in a productive way, she's swept up in a sea of contradictions and pulls Rick in along with her to ride the waves. When he comes close, she blasts him and rejects him.

These are three painful scenarios that could go very differently, perhaps even be avoided, if Karla, Craig, and Sheri were aware of how they're being unduly affected by their early relational programming and that their fear is really about things that happened long ago. If they each had a clue then,

- Karla might realize that the anxiety she was feeling about not hearing from Emily was triggered, in part, by past experiences. She might then be able to separate out her present truth from the distress-inducing shadows of the past and remind herself that, no matter what was going on with Emily, they'd deal with it and be okay.

- Craig might recognize that his defensiveness was in response to his own unmet needs for connection, a holdover from his childhood. If he were to get a little space from his distress, he could try to stay present long enough to learn that there's really nothing that he needs to be afraid of anymore. At the very least, he might apologize for getting defensive and try to get back on track with Lydia.

- Sheri might understand that the warring feelings inside her are not really an accurate reflection of her here and now experience, work to find a way to tame her distress, and not get pulled too far in any one direction. She might then be able to see herself and Rick more clearly and get a better sense of her feelings for him, as well as a more accurate sense of his actual feelings for her.

Instead Karla, Craig, and Sheri are all operating on autopilot, unconsciously playing out their early programming. Something happens for them that they perceive to be threatening, and their old relationship wiring gets activated, giving rise to familiar thoughts, feelings, and behaviors. It's predictable. From the outside looking in, we can hypothesize that they all had relationships with their caregivers in which they felt insecure and afraid and learned to respond in expectable ways. How can we tell? Their behaviors are characteristic of the typical relational patterns that people develop to adapt to their own early caregiving experiences and, thus, protect themselves in relationships. They're called "attachment styles."

Styles of Attachment

As infants, we are incredibly adaptive. We monitor our caregivers—their moods, emotional signals, and behaviors—and figure out how best to maximize the care we can get from them. *How do I need to cry? What expressions should I make or not make? What should I do if I'm angry, sad, or afraid? What will happen if I behave this way? How will they respond? What feelings should I express or not express? What aspects of me are okay and which are not? Which can I share freely and which do I need to hide?* Based on the ways in which we're responded to, we begin to get a sense of ourselves, others, and what we can expect. Accordingly we shape our behavior to fit our caretaking experiences. With repetition, patterns of behavior and the respective neural pathways that support these patterns get established in our brains and are strengthened over time.

What this means is that our internal working models of how to do relationships are developed through our early interactions with usually one or two people—our parents! And, although the cast of characters in our lives changes as we grow up and create lives for ourselves, the neural templates that govern our perceptions and emotional experience live on inside of us and continue to influence how we behave in our adult relationships. That's good news for those of us who had emotionally competent parents and not such good news for the many of us who didn't.

The lessons we learned about ourselves, about others, and about how to do relationships are reflected in our general patterns of relating, or attachment styles, of which, research shows, there are basically four types. Most people develop either a *secure, avoidant,* or *anxious* attachment style, while a few people develop what is called a *fearful-avoidant* attachment style. Let's take a look at each of them.

SECURE ATTACHMENT STYLE

If our parents were emotionally competent, that is, if they were sensitively attuned and consistently responsive to our emotional needs, if they made us feel safe, secure, and loved, we likely developed a *secure* attachment style. We learned that reaching out and connecting is a good thing and that we can trust and depend on our loved ones to be there for us when we need them. We learned that our feelings are not to be feared; rather they are our allies and are there to be helpful to us. We grow up to be adults who are comfortable with and adept at being close and connected with our loved ones. Our self-image is healthy, we feel worthy of love, and we view our partners in a positive light. We're emotionally available and responsive to our partners and can reach out to them for comfort and assurance when we're feeling vulnerable or distressed. When we have lapses, we can own our mistakes, take responsibility, and make repairs. Overall we're emotionally flexible; we can adapt to different situations and can easily flow between being close and connected with our partners to being comfortable on our own. Such is the case for more than half of the adults in the United States (US).

Then there are the rest of us.

AVOIDANT ATTACHMENT STYLE

When our caregivers are not attuned, distant, or intrusive, when they respond negatively or unreliably to our emotional needs, the seeds of insecurity get sown. We feel unsafe, anxious, and distressed, and in order to cope and maintain some degree of connection, we develop one of three insecure attachment styles of relating: *avoidant, anxious,* or *fearful-avoidant.*

Those of us with an *avoidant* attachment style, amounting to about 25 percent of the general (US) population, tend to have had parents who were emotionally unavailable, insensitive to and possibly rejecting of our emotional needs. As children, we sensed that our feelings and innate needs for connection were dangerous as they seemed to drive people away and that reaching out would only bring us rejection, criticism, disappointment, and pain. As a result, we learned to turn off or "deactivate" our natural needs for closeness. As adults, we find emotional intimacy threatening and prefer not to have anyone depend on us. We have a strong need to be independent and self-sufficient and to be seen as such.

While those with an avoidant attachment style tend to think positively of themselves, at least outwardly, they're wary of others, don't trust that they'll be there when needed, and frequently find fault with their partners. Although they may outwardly seem to have a positive perception of themselves, it may belie an underlying sense of insecurity. In spite of actually wanting to be close to another person, which is their natural inclination, they dismiss their emotional needs, deny their vulnerability, and keep their partners at arm's length. As you might have guessed, Craig, who got frustrated when his partner came to him seeking connection, has an avoidant attachment style.

ANXIOUS ATTACHMENT STYLE

Those of us who had caregivers who were inconsistently attuned to our feelings—at times nurturing and responsive and at other times insensitive, intrusive, or unavailable—likely developed this *anxious* attachment style. Such is the case for about 20 percent of the general adult population. Uncertain of what to expect from our caregivers, they had to work harder to get their attention. They learned to turn up the volume on or "hyper-activate" certain feelings to draw them in and, thus, maintain some degree of connection. They grow into adults who crave closeness but can't seem to get enough of it to quell their fears for any length of time. They wonder if their partners feel the same way they do and worry about whether they can believe or depend on their partners' love for them. Their relationships tend to be stressful, consuming their thoughts, and take up a lot of emotional real estate. They're highly sensitive to possible signs of rejection or abandonment and frequently seek reassurance and approval from their partners (which may work for a moment but, sooner or later, the worry and fear kick in again, and they're back in a spin cycle of anxiety and distress). They're easily upset, have strong emotional reactions, and can say or do things they later regret. They doubt their self-worth, tend to be self-critical, and have a hard time being on their own. Karla, who ruminated all day about whether her partner was angry or upset with her even though she had no real evidence to suspect this, has an anxious attachment style.

FEARFUL-AVOIDANT ATTACHMENT STYLE

A small number of us, about 5 percent, have a *fearful-avoidant* attachment style. Our caregivers likely had unresolved trauma of their own and, as a consequence, were emotionally unpredictable (for example, sometimes appropriately responsive, sometimes anxious or afraid, and sometimes behaving in ways that were frightening to us). As children, we couldn't be certain how they'd respond when we were distressed and were faced with an unsolvable dilemma: We needed soothing and connection from our attachment figure but feared the very person who should be providing it to us. Occasionally, our caregivers asked us to soothe them more than they were able to soothe us. Caught between a rock and a hard place, we resorted to a mixed bag of coping strategies that alternated between pushing our feelings down, amping them up, becoming compulsive caregivers, or checking out altogether. We grew into adults who, perhaps not surprisingly, have very ambivalent and conflicting feelings about emotional closeness. We both want and pursue connection, but then, when our partners seem to be moving closer to us, we get uncomfortable and pull back, afraid that we'll get hurt or be rejected, or we attack in order to reject them before they reject us. Our emotions often get the best of us, our moods can be erratic, and our relationships tend to be chaotic. We have a hard time communicating our feelings, think that we're flawed and unworthy of love, and view our partners negatively as being untrustworthy and possibly dangerous. Sheri, who both longs to be close to Rick but then freaks out and pushes him away when he tries to get closer to her, has a fearful-avoidant attachment style.

REFLECTION

As you read through the descriptions of the
different attachment styles, did you see yourself
in any one of them? Did you identify with any
particular style? Perhaps you see yourself as having
more of an anxious attachmen style. Maybe you
saw yourself as more avoidant in your relationships.
Maybe a little bit of each? You might even have
suspected that you have a fearful-avoidant style
of relating. If you found yourself identifying with
anything other than secure, you're not alone. When
it comes to romantic relationships, nearly half of us
have an insecure attachment style.

Now, before you start getting down on yourself, it's important to realize that these different categories are not rigid and discrete. The dividing lines that separate them are blurry, and there's overlap. The categories were originally developed for research purposes. Classifying individuals as having particular styles of relating benefits research by helping us to identify and understand common contributing factors like one's early experience in life and similar behavioral patterns and by enabling us to look at how these styles affect one's life experience. However, in reality there are many variations on a theme, so to speak. After all, we humans are a diverse lot with unique and varied histories and personal characteristics, all of which contribute to our experiences in life and how we operate in our relationships. In addition, our attachment style can also be affected by the attachment style of the person we are in relationship with. For instance, we might have more of an avoidant attachment style with one partner but respond with more of a fearful-avoidant attachment style if we are with a partner who experiences more attachment-related anxiety. Alternatively, we might have more of an anxious attachment style but have less attachment anxiety when we're with a partner who has a secure attachment style. So, we can think of each of the attachment styles as representing a range of possibilities within which we not only see similarities but also a fair amount of differences.

WHAT ABOUT TEMPERAMENT?

My mother would tell you that all three of her children were born with different personalities that were apparent from the moment we arrived. One of us was easygoing; one, more challenging; the third, more independent. (I won't out any of us here any further!) It's true all of us are born with natural dispositions, also known as "temperament." Our nervous systems are all a little different, and we each have innate tendencies to respond in unique ways. But, research has shown that temperament and attachment styles are not related. Rather, attachment styles develop from experience; they're something we acquire that are specific to each of our relationships with our parents. In other words, temperament is inborn, while attachment styles are learned.

A Matter of Degree

The work of Brennan, Clark, and Shaver helps to illustrate this point.[7] Based on their research, they created a graphic depiction of the attachment styles using two axes that represent two attachment-related dimensions: anxiety and avoidance. Essentially we can understand attachment styles as being determined by how comfortable or uncomfortable we are with intimacy, or how much we *avoid* it, and how *anxious* or preoccupied we are about our relationship and our partner's love for us.

Attachment Dimensions

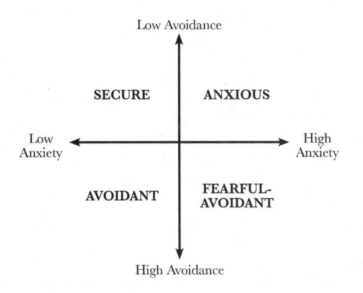

(Based on Brennan, Clark, and Shaver's Two Attachment Dimension Scale)

So, if you're comfortable with closeness and don't worry excessively about your relationship or your partner's love for you, you're likely secure. If you crave and enjoy closeness but fret a lot about your relationship and your partner's love for you, then you're likely anxious. If closeness and dependency make you uncomfortable, and you don't really worry or think a lot about your partner's commitment to your relationship, you're likely avoidant. And, if you're uncomfortable, with closeness, and you also worry about your partner's availability and love for you, you're likely fearful-avoidant. But, within each of the different attachment styles, there's quite a lot of variability when it comes to how comfortable you are with intimacy and how preoccupied you are about your relationship and your partner's love for you. The two dimensions or axes represent continuums of experience along which we have varying degrees of anxiety or avoidance. So, within each of these different attachment styles, we can have very different levels of comfort or distress. Therefore, while two people might have similar attachment styles, they can also differ quite a bit in the degree to which they're comfortable with intimacy and how concerned they are about their partner's availability and trustworthiness.

If you're still wondering what your attachment style might be and would like in-depth feedback, Dr. R. Chris Fraley, a leading attachment researcher at the University of Illinois, offers a free online adult attachment survey that you can take here: http://www.web-research-design.net/cgi-bin/crq/crq.pl.

How is This Helpful?

Keeping in mind that all of us are unique individuals, it helps to have an understanding of your general style of attachment. As you take a little step back and begin to observe yourself through an attachment-based lens, you can begin to see yourself more objectively. With some awareness of the behavioral patterns that are common for your attachment style, you're in a better place to recognize more readily when you're responding in a predetermined way, when the past is showing up in the present and unduly affecting your experience. Without this awareness, you're operating in the dark.

Remember, your style of relating is a result of the internal working models in your brain that operate on an unconscious level outside of our awareness. As psychologist Louis Cozolino explains, "our attachment schemas are implicit memories that are known without being thought."[8] In other words, you don't think, you just do. You don't realize that you're running on old programming that hasn't been updated for a new reality. You just keep responding from a place of fear even when there's really no reason to be afraid. You think, *This is just the way that I am,* and continue to do what you've done all along.

But, when you can recognize that you're responding in a habitual, predetermined way, you create an opportunity for change.

You can begin to see what needs to be rewired. You can have the option to start to do things differently.

Identifying the style in which you relate in your present life can give you insight into what your early experience with your caregivers was like. In turn, seeing why, when, and how these patterns originated in your past can help you make sense of your current behavior. So, you can trace a line from your current experience all the way back to when you were very young, and, conversely you can trace a line from your past to your present and begin to connect the dots.

○　○　○

To illustrate what I'm talking about, let's return to the stories of Craig, Karla, and Sheri, the clients whom you met at the beginning of this chapter.

In her relationship, why is Karla so anxious about not hearing from Emily? And, when she's finally in Emily's presence after a day of obsessing, why doesn't she just talk to her? Why doesn't she let Emily know that not hearing from her made her anxious, worried, or upset? Why, instead, does she sit sullenly starting at her dinner plate? The answers to these questions can be found in Karla's early experience in her family and the ways in which she adapted.

When I first asked Karla about her childhood, she painted a picture of her parents in broad strokes, remembering them as warm, loving, and supportive people. But, as we looked more closely, a different picture started to emerge, one that was marked by unpredictability and insecurity.

Karla eventually acknowledged that both of her parents were anxious people who vacillated between being overly involved with her or else consumed by their work. While they were sometimes present and engaged, there were times when they just didn't show up for her. One event, in particular, stood out in her mind and seemed to be emblematic of many others in which they weren't there for her when she needed them. On Karla's first day of school, arguably a momentous and an emotionally stressful day for any child, she was dropped off at school by a neighbor because her parents were busy with work and apparently unable to take her. Overcome with anxiety, Karla described feeling terrified and alone as she walked into the classroom, not knowing what to do nor what to expect. She silently walked to her desk staring at the floor, sat down, and anxiously awaited what would come next.

How does a child like Karla make sense of her parents' erratic presence? What does she make of them not being there for her when she needs them? Of her not seeming to warrant consistent care and attention? *Is it that I'm not important? Is there something wrong with me? Am I too much?* And, what does a child in such a situation come to expect of the important people in her life? *Can I rely on them? Can their love be trusted?* And what does she do to manage this scenario? How could she cobble together a modicum of security?

When Karla naturally asserted herself or expressed her fears, she was not always taken seriously. Instead her parents often questioned or minimized her feelings and told her, in so many words, that she should feel differently. However, one reliable thing that drew her parents in was when her mood turned sour, and she became sullen. Her parents leaned in with concern and distress, sometimes with frustration, not really attending to her feelings in a helpful way but at the very least, paying attention and engaging with her.

Connecting the dots from then to now, it's no wonder that Karla doesn't experience her relationship with Emily as secure and dependable, that she's on high alert for any sign that something might be off, that Emily might be slipping away or losing interest in her. Her early experience with her parents did not provide her with a sense of relationship security. Instead, it created within her an internal working model of relationships in which others were not to be trusted. It's no wonder she questions her own judgment and can't find her center, just as when she was questioned and not attuned to in a helpful way. And, it's no wonder that she can't directly express herself with Emily and, instead, turns sullen and withdrawn, relying on negative behaviors that garnered her parent's attention. That's how she learned to adapt.

What about Craig? Why is he so afraid of getting close to Lydia, allowing himself to be vulnerable, need connection, and depend on her? Why does he question her intentions and push her away? When I first began working with Craig, I learned that his early life was defined by a contentious divorce between his parents, his beloved mother going into overdrive to support the family, and his father being distant, unreachable, and argumentative. Out of fear of upsetting his parents and further fracturing his already broken family, Craig learned early on to put away his needs for closeness and care. He learned to be tough, to suppress his feelings, and thus to avoid the danger and pain of ever being hurt again.

Fast-forward to his present life, and Craig is still threatened by the prospect of closeness. He's still keeping his heart under tight wraps to avoid the pain his nervous system anticipates will ensue should he let himself be vulnerable and need Lydia. His internal working model for relationships dictates that his emotional needs are to be avoided since they'll only result in disappointment and despair.

How can we make sense of the competing feelings Sheri has? Of her longing for closeness and care but fearing it at the same time? Somewhere inside her is a little frightened girl, desperately needing a safe haven from a mother who was verbally and physically abusive at times, unpredictably coming at her like a "tornado" and berating her for illogical reasons, and a father who was often distant, callous, and rejecting. These were the same people who could sometimes demonstrate a modicum of kindness and caring. What did she learn to expect of others? What did she learn to expect of closeness? Is it safe, or is it dangerous? And what was she to do about this storm of feelings inside of her? She was trapped, in a bind, with no place to run and no place to hide. Her internal working model for relationships now gives her mixed messages. It's no wonder that getting close to someone, the very thing she longs for and desperately wants, causes her such distress.

Connecting the dots from then to now, Karla's, Craig's, and Sheri's current behaviors make more sense. They all did the best they could as children to make the most of their difficult situations. All three figured out what they needed to do to fit into and survive the little, unsafe worlds they initially inhabited. They learned their lessons well. And as they grew up, they hoped that someday things would be different, that they'd have relationships in which they'd feel safe and could be themselves, and in which their needs would be met. They expected that they just needed to meet the right person. But they didn't realize that they'd be operating on the same relationship programming from their childhood and, short of getting a software update, history would invariably repeat itself.

As I hope you're beginning to see, our attachment styles developed when we were very young and at the time they were adaptive. We saw and experienced life in a very basic, childlike way. We did the best we could to manage challenging situations, maintain some semblance of connection with our caregivers, and feel safe in environments that may not have been accepting of our emotional experiences and expression. We were just doing the best we could to get our needs met.

CONNECTING THE DOTS EXERCISE

Let's spend a little time trying to connect the dots between your current attachment style and your early experiences with your caregivers. Take a moment to read back over the descriptions of the different attachment styles. As you do, make note of any patterns of behavior or relational dynamics that sound familiar to you. Get a picture of the ways in which you typically respond to closeness, connection, or conflict in your relationship. With that in mind, trace a line back in time to when you were a child and see what you land on. How did your parents respond to your emotional needs?

What did you learn about yourself? What did you learn to expect from others? What did your child-self need to do to adapt? Then, trace a line back to your current life. How might some of your current behaviors simply be a continuation of those early adaptations? Can you see a relationship between your early experience and your behavior now? What's that like? What's it like to see the connection? How do you feel toward your child-self as you recognize how difficult and challenging things were for him or her? And how do you feel toward yourself now as you get a better understanding of how you were affected by your early experiences? As you reflect on what you've learned, offer yourself some kindness and appreciation for being willing to do this work.

It's All about Feelings, and Feelings in Relationships

Attachment styles represent categories of observable patterns of behavior, the ways in which we generally respond to connection and disconnection in our relationships. But our observable behavior is just the tip of the iceberg. While it helps to be able to recognize when we're playing out old patterns of behavior, that's not enough. If we're going to make a lasting change (and that's why we're here, isn't it?), we need to look at what's happening below the surface that's activating these patterns to begin with. We need to look at the emotional dynamics that are fueling how we respond. The relational strategies we typically resort to that constitute our attachment style are triggered by whatever feelings are getting stirred in us and the fear that these feelings engender.

As psychologist Diana Fosha, the developer of AEDP, explains in her book, *The Transforming Power of Affect*, attachment styles are basically strategies for dealing with emotion in relationships.[9]

Remember, we relate and connect with others through emotional experience, and our early relationships with our caregivers affect how we experience (or don't experience) our feelings. So the way in which we relate to others has everything to do with how we learned and continue to respond to our feelings, whatever they may be. Each attachment style has a particular pattern for dealing with emotions in relationships, especially when the feelings that get evoked are strong. Let's take another look at each of the styles but this time, through the lens of the emotional experience we have when we are in relationships.

SECURE ATTACHMENT STYLE OR "FEELING AND DEALING"

Those of us with a secure attachment style likely had parents who were emotionally competent. They were emotionally open, sensitive, and attuned to us, and consistently responded to our emotional needs in a balanced and helpful way. In turn, we developed emotional competency as well. That is, we learned to be mindful of, manage, and make good use of our feelings.

How does this kind of early life experience translate into how we navigate our adult relationships? We're attuned to both our own and our partner's emotions, are able to express ourselves in healthy ways, and can hang in and find our way through challenging situations together. In short, we're able to "feel and deal" no matter how difficult the feelings may be. We can experience and communicate our emotions while staying present and engaged with our partners in an emotionally mindful way.

AVOIDANT ATTACHMENT STYLE OR "DEALING BUT NOT FEELING"

Those of us with more of an avoidant attachment style most likely had parents who were uncomfortable with feelings, both theirs and ours. As such, they avoided their feelings, were emotionally unresponsive to us, and minimized our need for closeness and connection, whether indirectly or by actually saying things like, "Don't be a cry baby!" . . .

"You're so sensitive!" When we expressed ourselves or reached out in distress, they withdrew or shut down, leaving us feeling abandoned, rejected, and alone. As children, what were we to think? What were we to do? If acting on our innate desire to be emotionally open and connected brings us only disappointment, pain, and shame, then our feelings must be dangerous and avoided at all costs. Right? In order not to rock the boat and maintain some degree of connection with our caregivers, we learned to suppress and hide our feelings and our needs. Now as adults, we keep a tight wrap on our emotional experience, minimize our needs, and maintain a safe distance from others. When our comfort zone is encroached upon by a partner, when we start to feel vulnerable or have emotional needs, or when they do, we shut down or pull away. We dive into our work, play a round of video games, or go on a shopping spree. In short, we "deal but don't feel."

But I'm going to let you in on a little secret that many of you probably know already. While it may seem to others, and to ourselves for that matter, as though we're not having feelings or that we don't have needs for closeness, that's not really true. Somewhere deep inside of us our feelings and desire for connection are knocking at the door of our awareness trying to get our attention. But we can't hear them or don't want to hear them. The walls of our defenses are so thick that they muffle the sound as we keep ourselves distracted and cut off. Our anxiety and fear hide out behind our controlled demeanor and only start to show up when our self-imposed cage is rattled, and our feelings threaten to break out.

O   O   O

Craig, one of the clients you met earlier, is a master at dealing but not feeling. He's fine with the surface banter and joking nature of his interactions when his friends are around, but no sooner are he and Lydia alone, then he's reaching for his laptop trying to find safe cover. When Lydia draws near, and he's presented with the possibility of a more intimate connection with her, the hair on his back stands up. Feelings inside him start to stir, and he has to do something to extinguish the fire. He has to do something to keep them down, to keep them hidden, to get back to his safety zone. And so he lashes out and pulls away. He deals but doesn't feel. (Except that of course he does feel. But more about that later.)

ANXIOUS ATTACHMENT STYLE OR "FEELING BUT NOT DEALING"

If we identify with more of an anxious attachment style, we likely had caregivers who had difficulty regulating their own feelings and using them to good effect consistently. While they could sometimes be there for us when we were distressed, their own emotional anxiety and distress often got the best of them and interfered with their ability to respond reliably and be there for us in a helpful way. In fact, at times we might have even had to step into the role of caregiver and help them manage their own feelings. In this case, connection was for their needs first, for ours only secondarily.

Such emotional unpredictability raised our anxiety and led us to be hypersensitive to our parents' emotional state. We focused outward, vigilantly monitoring them for any signs of trouble, and in doing so lost touch with the depth of our own emotional experience. We had to work really hard to make contact with our preoccupied and self-involved parents and learned to overemphasize the feelings that more reliably got their attention, like unhappiness and distress.

As adults, we closely monitor our partner's emotional state and availability, pay a lot of attention to our own distress and disappointment, and are less aware of, or comfortable with, the other feelings we might be having. In general we have a hard time trusting, managing, and making good use of our emotions. Although it may appear as though we're in touch with our feelings, there's far too much anxiety and distress mixed in for them to be helpful. We can't land on any one feeling long enough to take advantage of its resources, and we end up feeling confused or conflicted. We're "emotional," but we're not able to get to the heart of our felt experience and move forward in a productive way. We feel, but we don't deal.

○ ○ ○

This is the story with Nora, who you met in Chapter One. She can argue a blue streak with her husband and complain about his lack of attention and interest, seemingly full of feeling, yet she's conflicted, afraid to let him see how vulnerable, afraid, and unworthy she feels inside, or to honor her anger and take a firm and steady stand. So she questions herself and keeps these feelings hidden, safely out of view. She "feels" but doesn't really deal.

Similarly, as you read at the start of this chapter, not hearing from Emily distresses Karla and she unknowingly turns up the volume on her unhappiness hoping that Emily will take the bait. Yet she's not able to see through the veil of her anxiety to discern what other feelings might be at play for her and to then lean in and address the matter with Emily in a healthy way. She too feels, but doesn't deal.

Neither of these women's actions help them get their needs met in any satisfying way and their true feelings remain obstructed by their distress.

FEARFUL-AVOIDANT ATTACHMENT STYLE OR "NOT FEELING, OR REELING, AND NOT DEALING"

Those of us with a fearful-avoidant attachment style had caregivers who weren't able to regulate their own feelings and sometimes acted in ways that frightened us. Confused and afraid, and with no one to turn to soothe our fears and protect us, we were overwhelmed by a conflictual mix of feelings. We didn't learn how to manage and move through our emotional experience. Instead, we either went numb or were overcome by the force of our emotions and fell apart. As adults, we have trouble modulating our feelings and are often overwhelmed by them, especially when a partner or love interest tries to get close. Unable to manage our emotions and stay present when we're distressed or upset, we either check out (dissociate) or get swept up in an emotional storm (as in "reeling"), never getting to the root of our problems or figuring out a way forward. We don't feel or we reel, and despite our best efforts in either case, we don't deal.

This is what's happening for Sheri, whom you also met at the start of this chapter. She longs for closeness and connection, but it also wigs her out. When Rick leans in and gets serious, she can't stay present. She's unable to manage the swirl of feelings that erupt inside her, so she spins out of control. She reels and doesn't deal.

REFLECTION

As you read over these different strategies for dealing with emotion, which sound familiar to you? How do you typically respond to your feelings in your relationship? Take a moment to think about it. Are you more prone to minimize, dismiss, or detach from your feelings or from your partner? Do you have a strong need to be in control? Do you often not know how you feel? Do you frequently get upset and have a hard time getting to the other side of your feelings? Do you pay more attention to your partner's feelings than to your own? Are certain feelings okay and others not? Do your feelings get the best of you and seem to run the show? Are you feeling and dealing, or are you doing something else?

These are hard questions to consider but ever so important. Give yourself some credit for hanging in and being willing to take an honest look at yourself. You're setting yourself up to be able to make good use of the tools that we will soon learn.

As with the attachment styles, we can think of these different ways of coping with our feelings in our relationships as representing a broad range of strategies. Strategies that we might all resort to at some time or another, regardless of our general attachment style.

The truth is, all of us can feel emotionally insecure or overwhelmed at times and behave in ways that are unproductive.

When we don't feel and deal, it's inevitable that certain feelings get distorted or excluded from our emotional experience. When this happens, our capacity to function in healthy ways is compromised, and our core self is lost to our anxiety. Remember, our feelings are there to help us. It's impossible to have a healthy and satisfying relationship if parts of our emotional experience are distorted or left out. And when we don't realize what we're doing, when we don't realize what's going on inside of us, we don't have a choice.

It's the undoing of these emotional dynamics and the creation of new ones that is the key to ultimately having the kinds of relationships we really want. When we can find a way to stay present and deal with our experience, we can find a way to a better relationship. How to do just that will be our focus for the rest of this book.

Updating the Wiring

Although attachment styles and the underlying emotional dynamics can remain fairly stable over time—especially in the context of a long-term relationship—*they are not immutable*. We don't have to remain prisoners to our past programming. We can update our internal working models and change our styles of relating. We can change the way we react to our feelings and develop what is called an "earned secure" attachment style. Remember, even though we're wired to respond in a certain way, our brain is still able to change and grow—a capacity known as "neuroplasticity." With focused attention and practice, we can build new brain circuitry that supports other ways of relating. We can develop the emotional capabilities that secure connections with our caregivers would have afforded us and change our attachment styles. We can reclaim the richness of our emotional experience and bring a more fully integrated and resourced self—our core self—to our relationships.

Knowing your attachment style and how you respond to your emotional experience can help bring these dynamics into conscious awareness. It will help you to identify when you're responding in a programmed way, when your current emotional capacity is being unduly affected by old neural wiring, and when your past is overshadowing your present experience. As you begin to observe your emotional dynamics and identify what's going on for you, you can start to disentangle yourself from your old nervous system responses and begin to do things differently. To quote renowned psychiatrist and author of *The Mindful Brain*, Daniel J. Siegel, "When we can name it, we can tame it."[10]

As with any situation you're afraid of, the more you avoid it, the less opportunity you have for facing and overcoming your fears. If you continue to avoid expressing your feelings, you'll never know what good can come from sharing them; you'll never see that they really aren't something you need to fear. You'll just keep doing the same thing over and over again. You'll keep traveling down those old neural pathways that get you nowhere.

To change, you need to make a concerted effort to travel in a different direction. You need to find a way to recognize and tame your outmoded fear, stay present with, and sort through your emotional experience, and start opening up and sharing your feelings, needs, and desires in a new and constructive way.

Over time, the more you move in this different direction, the more you'll develop your capacity to be emotionally present, open up, and communicate what's inside of you. Your fear will shrink in size and you'll soon be able to stay present and share your feelings without feeling anxious or overwhelmed. And while you're doing this, you're actually rewiring your brain. You're breaking the old associations between fear and emotional connection and creating new, updated, mental models of relating in which sharing your feelings is now recognized and experienced as something beneficial.

In the next chapter, we'll take a look at what happens when your old programming gets activated, and you'll get started building your emotional mindfulness skills.

CHAPTER TAKEAWAYS

- Our early experiences with others create internal working models that shape our sense of self, of others, and of what we can expect in relationships.

- We develop different attachment styles, or ways of relating to others, based on our early experience with our caregivers.

- Two dimensions—how comfortable we are with intimacy and how anxious we are about our relationships—determine our attachment style.

- Attachment styles can be viewed as strategies for dealing with emotion in relationships.

- Attachment styles are not immutable but can be changed through intention, practice, and new experiences. We can develop an "earned secure" style of attachment.

- Your attachment style can give you insights into what your early experience with your caregivers was like, and vice versa.

- Knowing your attachment style can help you better understand yourself and how you typically respond to your feelings in your relationships.

- When you're not able to feel and deal with your emotions in your relationships, your capacity to function is compromised.

- When you are able to observe your emotional dynamics, you can disentangle yourself from your fears and begin to do things differently.

PART II:

Updating Our Wiring

CHAPTER THREE

Step One: Recognize and Name

*"Awareness is like the Sun.
When it shines on things, they are transformed."*
—THICH NHAT HANH

Sophie was on a tear. Pulling clothes from the closet, trying them on, taking them off in fits of exasperation, the bedroom littered with an array of rejected outfits. Her interview was less than an hour away and she couldn't find anything to wear that felt right. *I'm such a basket case*, she thought to herself. And then, with more than a note of sarcasm: *This is really going to go well!*

Sophie had woken up that morning feeling out of sorts and it just kept getting worse. Was it the interview that was making her feel so stressed? It would be a big deal to get this position. But isn't that what she wanted? She had been looking forward to this interview for a while, and although it made her a little nervous when she thought about it, up until last night she'd been feeling excited.

Was it something else?

On the surface, everything seemed fine in Sophie's life. Her career was moving along, she'd been enjoying her friends, and most importantly, things were going well with her boyfriend, Mike. In fact, at his suggestion they'd been talking about moving in together. Sophie loved that Mike had initiated the conversation on his own and seemed eager to take the next step in their relationship. It's what she had been hoping for. Then last night when Sophie casually mentioned that she saw a "for rent" sign on a building two blocks over from where she was living now, Mike seemed aloof.

"Should I call and see when we can look at it?" Sophie tentatively asked.

"Sure," Mike replied, half-heartedly.

A twinge of panic flashed in Sophie's chest, and she got a sick feeling in her stomach. But it was her worries that captured her attention. *Is he having second thoughts?* she wondered. *Did I do something to upset him? Is he mad at me?* Her thoughts quickened as she played over the last few days in her mind, searching for a clue. They'd just had a fun weekend away together and Mike had been so sweet and caring. But ever since they'd gotten back to town, Sophie had felt a bit on edge, worried that something bad might happen. *What if it doesn't work out? What if he changes his mind?*

She wanted to tell him she was feeling vulnerable and wished he would say or do something to reassure her. Show her some sign that everything was fine between them. But she couldn't bring herself to say anything, worried that she might annoy him, that she'd seem too needy or desperate. Instead, hoping Mike would snap out of the haze he seemed to be in, she tentatively asked, "Um, are you okay?"

"Yeah. Sure. I'm just tired," he said, yawning. "I should get ready for bed."

"Um, me too, I guess." Sophie said with a feigned smile as she watched Mike get up and go into the bedroom. She sat silently on the couch for a moment, disappointed, anxious, confused. *He's had a long day*, she told herself, trying to shake off her distress. *But he's staying over tonight, so that's a good sign. Right? Why am I getting too worked up over this?* She took a breath and tried to put the whole thing out of her mind.

Yet the feelings rumbled on inside her, disrupting her sleep. Sophie woke up the next day, bleary-eyed and irritable, and as the morning quickly passed, she found herself feeling annoyed with Mike. *Why did he have to stay here the night before my interview? I would have slept better and had the morning to get ready on my own. Now look at me!* she thought as she angrily buttoned her shirt.

Mike sauntered in the room, dressed and ready for work. "What's the matter?" he asked, sensing that something was wrong. "Are you okay?"

"No, I'm not okay!" She snapped in frustration, heading back to the closet. Then, startled by the force of her own feelings, she tried to soften the edge in her voice and offered, "I don't know. I just . . . I just hate how I look."

"What are you talking about?" Mike said. "You look great!"

Sophie turned to look at him for a brief moment, tears of distress welling in her eyes, and then hurried to gather her things. She realized she'd somehow failed to see the look of compassion on Mike's face. "I don't know. I guess I'm more nervous about this interview than I thought," she said as she hurried past him and headed for the door.

○ ○ ○

From the outside looking in, this might seem like an easily avoidable situation. If Sophie would just talk with Mike and share with him that she feels anxious that he may be getting cold feet about moving in together, perhaps he might reassure her that everything is okay. Or maybe he'd admit that he was slow to respond because *he* is feeling nervous. After all, moving in together can be anxiety provoking for a couple, no matter how great things are going. Or maybe he has an avoidant attachment style and closeness feels threatening to him. In any case, they'd be in a much better place to navigate the feelings that are coming up for them.

We can't constructively deal with our emotions unless we recognize and pay attention to them. But Sophie feels conflicted about her feelings. She questions and doubts herself, tries to dismiss her fear, and then, invariably, erupts in a tangled mix of distress, anger, and hurt. Not at all a recipe for getting her needs met. Not at all a recipe for getting back to good with Mike.

You might have guessed that Sophie has an anxious attachment style. In general, it's hard for her to trust in the security of her relationship as the threat of possible abandonment looms large in her psyche. She learned early on in life that loved ones won't be there reliably when she needs them and suspects that, sooner or later, she'll do something to upset the applecart and everything will fall apart. So when Mike fails to respond with total enthusiasm to her mention of the available apartment, her nervous system jumps to attention. Her brain sends out a warning signal that she's in danger, and her old emotional programming takes over.

While the manner in which Sophie behaves might seem a bit extreme, at its core her fear is quite universal. As you know, our need for a secure connection with a loved one is innate, wired in by millions of years of evolution. Any sign of a potential loss of connection with a romantic partner can stir fear in us. If we sense that something is awry in our relationship, our attachment system gets activated—our needs for safe connection come online, and we're inclined to reach out and makes things better. That's how we're wired.

Those of us with a secure attachment style experience such moments as if they're just bumps in the road that we're able to navigate, and then get back on track with our partners. We feel our feelings and respond in a healthy way. But for those of us with an insecure attachment style, our early experiences in life mucked with our emotional wiring. Consequently, we're not only hypersensitive to emotional cues in our relationships, we have a sort of phobic response to the feelings that they engender in us.[1,2] We react to them as though they're dangerous. Emotions begin to stir in us, and without us knowing it, our nervous system gets activated and, for better or worse, we respond to our feelings and their associated needs and desires as our early history conditioned us to respond.

○   ○   ○

Sophie has no clue as to what's going on for her. She doesn't realize that she's been triggered—that an emotional hot button has been pushed and her old programming is running the show. If she did, she might understand that more than Mike's response, it's her fear that's getting the best of her. Perhaps she'd recognize she was falling into well-worn patterns of behavior and responding defensively. She might then handle her feelings and the situation very differently. But unaware of what's happening for her emotionally, she doesn't have a choice. She's powerless.

That's how it goes for many of us. We don't recognize when we've been triggered internally. We get so swept up in our reaction that we can't see what's actually going on. We don't notice or understand the underlying dynamics that are driving our emotional experience. We don't get that the activation of our nervous system is a blast from the past and as such has little to do with what we're facing in the present moment. And when something happens that disconfirms our assumption, like Mike's look of compassion, we disregard it.

If we're going to be able to turn things around, we need to recognize when we've been triggered. We need to slow ourselves down and start paying attention to what's going on inside of us. We need to become intimately acquainted with and adept at recognizing and handling the forces inside of us. In short, we need to develop our capacity for emotional mindfulness.

Emotional Mindfulness

I'm guessing that "mindfulness" is a term you've heard. While the practice of mindfulness has been around for thousands of years, it's been getting a lot of airtime lately. In recent years, it's made the front page of the *New York Times*, the cover of several major magazines, and was the featured topic on a number of popular talk shows. Just scan an online news feed and I'm sure you'll come across an article that makes some reference to mindfulness. Why is that? One reason likely has to do with the mental and emotional cost of living in an age of digital distraction and social unrest. While technology has certainly enhanced our lives in many ways, the steady barrage of emails, text messages, and distressing news updates, all vying for our attention at once, can be overwhelming and stressful. Many of us are seeking a way to quiet the buzz of our overstimulated nervous systems, regain some sense of equanimity in our lives, and focus on what's important.

Yet the primary reason we're hearing a lot about mindfulness these days likely has more to do with a veritable explosion of research findings attesting to its many benefits. Study after study is showing that practicing mindfulness improves our physical, mental, and social well-being. In particular, it's been proven to be effective in reducing stress, rumination, and emotional reactivity, and to enhance immune functioning, insight, intuition, the ability to focus, cognitive flexibility, compassion, and relationship satisfaction.[11] Sounds like something to consider!

What then are we talking about when we refer to mindfulness? That's a good question. Depending on the context and who you're talking to, mindfulness can take on different meanings, and that has led to some misunderstandings. Fundamentally, and for our purposes, mindfulness is about paying attention to our present moment experience in an accepting, nonjudgmental manner. It involves actively focusing on our unfolding experience—sensing, observing, and allowing—without having to change it or respond in any particular way. It's about accepting what is and allowing it to be.

The practice of mindfulness seeks to strengthen our capacity for focused attention and increase our conscious awareness. By "paying attention on purpose"[12] with acceptance, we come to see that all experience is transient and constantly changing and, if we face and stay present to it, eventually passes. We come to see that when we stay open to our experiences, we can move through them and get to a better place. It frees us from being wedded to the past or worrying about the future and enables us to be more wholly present and engaged in the here and now.

One common misconception about mindfulness is that it's about getting in a zone in which we're not affected by anything, impervious to the vicissitudes of life. Well that's just not true, nor is it even desirable. As emotional beings, we are wired to feel. If we didn't, our lives would be devoid of energy, color, and richness. What would be the point of that?

Mindfulness is not about achieving some detached way of being. That would be deadening. Rather it's about finding a healthy balance between experiencing and observing what's happening for us without being pulled too far in any one direction—a stance that's been referred to as "participatory-observation." It's about getting different regions of our brain—the emotional part and the thinking part—to work together.

When we are mindful, we are more integrated. We can both feel and see more clearly what we're experiencing and how we're habitually inclined to react. We can more readily recognize when we've been triggered and manage our experience without being forced to play out conditioned patterns of responding that are no longer helpful to us. We can get ourselves unhooked.

Practicing mindfulness leads to greater self-awareness and psychological flexibility. It cultivates mental space within us, enabling us to gain a larger, more open-minded perspective, and consider how best to respond to our experience. Our range of options broadened, we are freer to make wiser choices that are more aligned with how we want to be.

Moreover, when we intentionally focus our attention on practicing new and positive behaviors, we are practicing what neuroscientist Jeffrey Schwartz aptly calls, "self-directed neuroplasticity."[13] We're harnessing the brain's capacity to rewire itself so that it can work on our own behalf. We're updating our neural circuitry. In a way, as psychologist Rick Hanson suggests, we're using our minds to change our brains.[14]

"Emotional mindfulness," as the phrase implies, is mindfulness with a particular emphasis on our emotional experience. Remember, while our early relational wiring is evident in the ways in which we respond to our feelings, the whole process is largely unconscious. We don't realize what's going on inside of us—that we're having feelings and responding to them in unhelpful ways. We don't realize that we've been triggered, and internal working models for dealing with our emotions in our relationships have taken over. But we need to. The way out of this trap is through attending to our emotional experience.

Practicing emotional mindfulness serves as an antidote to our struggles by helping us to see and shift the emotional dynamics that have been unconsciously governing our behavior more readily. It grows our awareness of our feelings and increases our capacity to abide and work constructively with them. In turn, we're better able to regulate our distress and objectively see and respond to what's happening within us and before us. When we approach our practice with a healthy dose of kindness and compassion for ourselves, it makes it easier for us to deal with whatever we may encounter.[15]

When we are mindful, we are freed up to develop new ways of relating to ourselves and to others. When we are mindful, we can love, and be loved, like we mean it.

Sounds good, huh? It is, but just as it is when we're learning any new skill, it takes some work. After all, we've been unknowingly responding to our emotions in a particular way for a long time, so those patterns have become entrenched and automatic. They're well-worn paths that we travel down without even thinking. It takes some effort to get and keep things moving in a different direction. But the more we practice them, the better our abilities become.

To that end, some people find that developing a daily meditation practice helps them to grow their mindfulness skills more readily. It does. But while meditating regularly is immensely helpful in that regard, and I highly recommend it, it isn't the only way. Practicing emotional mindfulness can be done anytime and anywhere. In fact, research shows that repeated experiences in small doses—"little and often"—is what builds strong neural pathways in our brains.[16] With intention and skill, we can repeatedly take a few minutes throughout our day to build and strengthen our emotional mindfulness circuitry. All we need to do is bring our attention to our felt experience and be with it, over and over again.

The four steps that I teach are all about growing our capacity for emotional mindfulness. They are:

Step One: Recognize and Name

Step Two: Stop, Drop, and Stay

Step Three: Pause and Reflect

Step Four: Mindfully Relate

We begin with Step One, "Recognize and Name," which is about cultivating our awareness and ability to observe our present-moment experience. The main goal in this step is to become mindful of times when an emotional hot button gets pushed and our old programming takes over. In order to be able to do things differently, we need to see what's happening for us emotionally when it's occurring. After all, we can't change something we're not aware of. We need to be able to recognize when we've been triggered and label it as such. As the saying goes, we need to name it so that we can tame it.

To that end, let's get an understanding of what's going on under the hood when we get triggered.

A Hijacking of Sorts

Evolution has programmed us to be on the lookout for danger. Without us knowing it, our amygdala—the "threat detector" that we talked about earlier and one of the oldest and more primitive parts of the brain—is constantly scanning our environment to assess our level of safety and alert us to signs of trouble. It's a basic survival mechanism with the goal of protecting us and keeping us safe. It was especially useful to us in prehistoric times when the threat of physical danger loomed large. Because of its central location and the way our brains are wired, the amygdala can bypass the prefrontal cortex, the "executive center" and more newly evolved part of our brain, and rapidly alert the body to danger. When trouble's afoot, the amygdala "hijacks" our brain and we spring into action before we're even aware of what's going on.

Here's what happens: When our amygdala detects that we may be in harm's way, it sends out a distress signal, our nervous system gets activated, stress hormones like adrenaline and cortisol get released, and our body is put on high alert. The sympathetic branch of our nervous system, an accelerator of sorts, revs us up and readies our body to fight off a threat or flee to safety—the "fight-flight-or-freeze" response. Our awareness heightens, our breathing quickens, our muscles tense up, and we take action. Or when escape from danger seems impossible, our body shuts down, and we become immobilized as a way of protecting ourselves. In any case, the whole process happens in a flash, before our slower moving prefrontal cortex weighs in with an assessment of the meaning and significance of the situation. When it's clear to our brain that we're no longer in danger ("Ha! That's a twig, not a snake!") the parasympathetic branch of our nervous system steps on the brakes, and our system calms down and returns us to a state of rest.

The amygdala's ability to hijack our brain is a nifty trick when our survival is dependent on our being able to respond in a flash and without thinking. I know I'm grateful for its talents when, seemingly out of nowhere, I find myself slamming on my car's brakes and avoiding a near accident (and a costly trip to the repair shop, for that matter). I'm willing to wager a bet that you do as well!

But in general the kinds of "threats" we encounter in our modern-day lives are more symbolic (like someone cutting in front of us in line, getting dissed by a coworker, or an angry look on our partner's face), than the life-threatening scenarios our early ancestors faced (cue the saber-toothed tiger). Unfortunately, our amygdala isn't so great at telling the difference, and we get thrown into survival mode when it's not really warranted. Here's where our rapid-fire, nonthinking response to a perceived threat can be a liability, especially when it comes to navigating our emotional experiences in our relationships.

Remember, our amygdala perceives threats based on past experience. When we start to have certain feelings, needs, or desires with our partners, and our experience is similar in any way to emotionally charged memories of situations in which we got negative responses in our early lives, we get triggered. Regardless of whether our perception is accurate, our amygdala sounds the alarm that we're in danger, our nervous system responds accordingly, and our defenses spring into action. Although the original threat of loss (and death) no longer exists, we respond as though it does and become unwitting contributors to our own suffering.

Minding the Gap Between Impulse and Action

When you met Sophie at the beginning of this chapter, she was missing the initial cues that she's been triggered by her boyfriend's lukewarm response to the idea of looking at an apartment for the two of them. Within a heartbeat her old programming was up and running.

Like Sophie, when we're triggered we go from stimulus to response in a nanosecond. A button gets pushed and our default programming takes over. It all happens so quickly. But if we could slow things down, if we could widen the gap between impulse and action, we'd afford ourselves some necessary space to be able to do things differently.

The key to being able to do just that lies in aligning with our prefrontal cortex, which resides in the upper part of our brain. The prefrontal cortex has been likened to an orchestra conductor. It oversees all the different "players" and gets them to work together to create beautiful music. Similar to a conductor's ability to guide, balance, and shape the sounds coming from different sections of the orchestra, the prefrontal cortex has the capacity to calm our amygdala, regulate our nervous system, and say "no" to instinctive survival responses—essential skills for navigating the emotional terrain of our relationships.

But the top-down neural connections that run from our prefrontal cortex or "higher brain" to the subcortical regions or "lower brain" where our amygdala resides are not as strong as the bottom-up connections that run in the other direction. That's how the amygdala can so easily get the upper hand. That's how we're designed. Fortunately, our top-down circuitry can be strengthened and we can tip the balance in our favor. Mindfulness helps us do just that by strengthening our capacity for self-observation.

We can enlist the help of our prefrontal cortex intentionally by bringing our "observer" online. Our observer is the part of us that's able to see, watch, and identify what's happening. It's not thinking, it's not assessing or judging, it's just watching. For instance, imagine gently holding your experience in an outstretched hand where you can examine it in front of you. You can turn your hand to consider it from different angles. When we observe and describe our experience, we create a little space between us and it. Instead of being completely absorbed in our distress, we step out of it just enough so that we can turn and look at it more objectively. We can then identify and name our emotional experience, which also helps to shift the power back to our prefrontal cortex. By using our higher brain to manage our lower brain, so to speak, we can more accurately see what's happening in the moment and avoid being controlled by our old programming.

When we're triggered, we're at risk of getting overwhelmed and helpless to do anything about it. Observing changes our relationship with our emotional experience. It becomes something that's happening for us rather than the totality of who we are. We can look at our feelings without being unduly affected by them. In the doing, we not only change our relationship with our feelings, but our experience itself changes as well.

So where do we start when it comes to observing our emotional experience? And how do we make sense of what we're observing? There is a tool that I would like to share with you now that can help us do just that.

Through the Lens of a Triangle

Ever since I began my training as a psychologist, I've been interested in understanding how best to help people change. While I've gained a lot of insight and skill over the years, one tool stands out as being foundational to my work and informs everything I do. Now you might think that something so significant would be a complex concept or intervention, but the funny thing is it's actually just a simple diagram.

"The Triangle of Experience," or what we'll call "the Triangle" for short, is a graphic depiction of our internal working models for dealing with emotion in relationships, the programming that's been governing our experience. By illustrating what happens when anxiety-provoking feelings, needs, or desires get activated in us, the Triangle shines the light of awareness on what's been going on behind the scenes. While the Triangle has been invaluable to me in my efforts to understand people's struggles and help them overcome the fear they have of their feelings, many of my clients have been helped by learning about it as well. By identifying and graphically separating out the main aspects of their emotional experience and then illustrating how they relate to one another, the Triangle helps them to see and make sense of their emotional dynamics. It provides a lens through which they can step back and observe what is happening for them on a moment-to-moment basis. In turn, they're better able to notice when they've been triggered and identify what's happening for them. They're able to interrupt the process and get back in the driver's seat instead of being blindly taken for a ride. That's precisely why I'm sharing it with you.

First let me give you the lay of the land. As you can see in Figure 1 on the next page, each corner of the Triangle represents one of the three main components of our emotional experience—our feelings, anxiety, and defenses. These are the elements of our experience that we need to be on the lookout for and be able to identify.

In the bottom corner are our core feelings, along with their inherent needs and desires (F). Their position at the bottom of the Triangle makes intuitive sense as our emotional truth often resides somewhere deep inside of us, and thus arises from our core—from the "bottom up." It also speaks to the innate, wired-in aspect of our emotions and needs for connection, love, and safety.

Figure 1

THE TRIANGLE

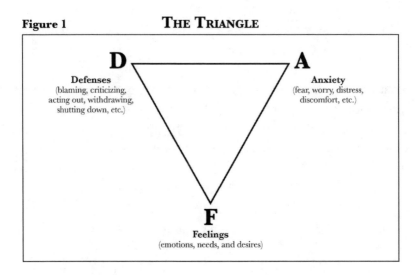

The upper right-hand corner (A) represents the anxiety, fear, and distress that through our early experiences with our caregivers became associated with our core emotions, needs, and desires. (To simplify things, we'll refer to all these feelings under the rubric of "anxiety.")

On the left-hand side (D) are our defenses, which are all the thoughts, behaviors, and reactions we've developed to protect ourselves and manage the anxiety our emotions have come to engender. These are coping strategies that we use to "defend" against our core emotional experience; they try to hide or keep feelings at bay. It's our defenses and anxiety that tell us when we've been triggered. Their location at the top of the Triangle indicates how in real life they occur on the surface and cover or mask our core emotions.

Figure 2 illustrates what happens when we get emotionally triggered. Let's walk through the process step by step.

Figure 2   **THE TRIANGLE IN ACTION**

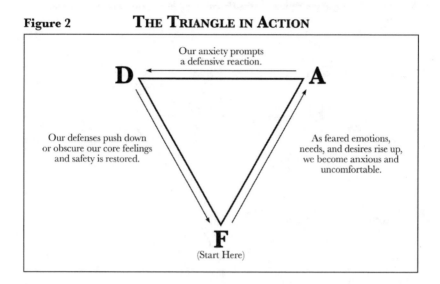

In relationships, something happens that gets our attention and evokes an emotional response in us. It could be any number of things—a thought, comment, look, or tone of voice, the lack of a response when we try to connect, our partner seeming upset or indifferent, and so on. If the emotion, need, or desire that then gets evoked is one that we learned to fear, our amygdala sounds the alarm that danger is drawing near. Our nervous system gets activated, our body responds, and we feel uncomfortable (A). As our distress increases it prompts us to do something, anything, to restore a sense of safety. Our defenses rush to the scene and mount a counterattack by either pushing our feelings back down or amping up other, more "acceptable" feelings (D). In either case, our core emotions, needs, and desires get suppressed or distorted just enough so that the associated fear dissipates, and for a moment "safety" is restored. That is, until we start to experience another anxiety-inducing feeling, and the whole pattern repeats itself. Maybe not with the same defenses, but with the same triangular dynamic.

o o o

Let's come back to Sophie's story to illustrate what this process looks like in real life.

Figure 3   SOPHIE'S EMOTIONAL DYNAMICS

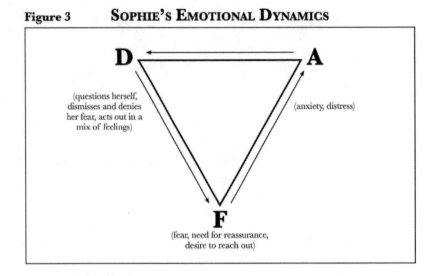

When Mike has a lackluster response to Sophie's suggestion that they check out an apartment together, these dynamics get set in motion. A wave of fear rises up inside Sophie along with a desire to reach out for comfort and get reassurance from Mike that all is well (F). With that, an alarm bell goes off inside her to warn her that she's moving into dangerous waters, and she then feels anxious and conflicted (A). "No, no, no, don't let him know what you're feeling!" her implicit memory, shaped by her early thwarted attachment attempts, reminds her. "You know where that will go!" With that, Sophie begins to question her feelings, tries to shrug them off and act like she's fine (D). In turn, her anxiety lowers a bit but keeps threatening to break through. Finally, when she can no longer contain herself, she acts out in a jumbled mix of anger, hurt, and distress (D). What's important to recognize here is that the feelings she acts out— anger and hurt—although they are feelings, are not her core feelings. Rather, they are defenses against her core emotional experience of feeling afraid and desiring reassurance, connection, and closeness.

And there you have it: a bird's-eye view of Sophie's emotional programming, the neural coding of her early conditioning laid bare in black and white. Sophie's Triangle reveals an internal working model that prevents her from expressing her true feelings. If Sophie was able to back up a bit and observe what was going on for her, she might recognize a familiar pattern. She might notice that she's been triggered and how she's inclined to respond. She might recognize when she's getting defensive, rein herself back in, and try something different. At the very least, she might be able to make some sense of what happened to her.

With the Triangle, she can do all of these things—as can you. First, you can use it as a frame of reference to help you make sense of your emotional experience. Sketch out a Triangle on a piece of paper and try mapping out some of your relationship experiences on it. Try to observe your interactions through the lens of the Triangle—noting when you're having feelings, seeing when your anxiety arises, and recognizing how you're inclined to respond in a defensive manner.

The more you do it, the more you'll be able to parse out the different elements of your experience and identify what's been going on for you. Next you can see and name what's happening. For instance, you can say, "I just got triggered," or "I'm getting defensive," or "I'm feeling hurt."

This step is actually quite powerful. As research by psychologist Matthew Lieberman and his colleagues has shown, labeling our emotional experience gets our prefrontal cortex engaged and calms down our amygdala.[17] It helps to regulate our nervous system and makes it easier for us to get unhooked and think through how best to handle the situation.[18]

When we recognize and name what's happening for us, we're bringing in a dose of reality. We're separating out our past from the present moment and helping ourselves see it with clear eyes. In addition, when we repeatedly note and name our emotional experience, we start to see our patterns of behavior more clearly. We come to more readily see how and when we've gotten hooked and begin to do things differently in our relationships.

That's a loving thing to do. We're attending to ourselves in the way in which an attuned and caring parent would attend to a child and help them with their feelings. But what are we looking for? What are the cues that tell us we're feeling anxious? How can we tell if we're in a defensive mode? How do we know if we're in touch with our core feelings? That's where we turn our attention next.

Getting a Clue

When Sophie got triggered, she experienced a wave of panic and got a sick feeling in her stomach. Her attention went straight to her thoughts, where she ended up trapped in the spin cycle. She was not aware of what was going on for her.

Awareness—knowing that something is happening when it's happening—is a central component of mindfulness. The key to growing our *emotional* awareness lies in becoming more attuned to what's going on in our bodies. Why? Because that's where our feelings show up. They make their presence known through energy, sensations, and visceral reactions that register in our bodies, and we feel them. If we didn't have a body, we wouldn't have feelings. Mindfully tuning into bodily sensations increases our conscious awareness of our feelings, keys us into important information, and helps to reveal our core emotional experience.

Similar to Sophie, many of us are not accustomed to paying attention to what's going on inside of us. We're consumed by our thoughts, caught up in our distress, or focused solely on what's going on in front of us. As such, we're alienated from our felt experience. That's a problem. When we're not aware of what's going on inside us we're completely at the mercy of our faulty wiring.

But if we grow our awareness, if we become more attuned to our internal experience and can recognize when we've been triggered and are having feelings, we can turn things around.

So then, what's it like for you when you get triggered? What are the signs? Here's where the Triangle can help you sort out your experience. Remember, you get triggered when conflicting feelings, needs, or desires—the stuff at the bottom of the Triangle—start to come up. As you proceed through the four steps, you'll be better able to recognize your core emotional experience as it's emerging, but given how fast the alarm bell gets rung and your nervous system takes over, at this point in your process you're more likely to get uncomfortable and fly right into defense mode. So it's the stuff at the top of the Triangle—feeling anxious or behaving in a defensive manner—that you need to catch.

The ability to recognize both is important. They're both indicators that you've been triggered. But if you can spot your anxiety when it first arises, it's a little easier to slow things down and regain some control. By the time you're in defense mode and up to your old tricks, it can be a bit challenging, although certainly not impossible, to rein yourself in.

For that reason, let's focus first on being able to recognize when anxiety appears on the scene.

The "A" Corner of the Triangle

Physical discomfort is often the first sign that we're anxious and that our nervous system is reacting as though we're in danger. It's telling us that we're starting to have an emotional experience that our amygdala suspects will put us in danger. For instance, we begin to feel hurt, afraid, angry, in need of reassurance or support, or we feel compelled to express ourselves in some way, and the alarm bell starts to sound. In turn, we feel anxious, afraid, or distressed. We feel physically uncomfortable. It's unpleasant. Why? Because it's a threat signal. It's trying to get our attention. It wants to get us to do something. If it made us feel all warm and fuzzy inside, we'd relax and settle in, but that's not what anxiety's about. Instead, the suffering it generates makes us want to do something to put an end to it, to make it go away.

Now with all this talk of alarms going off, you'd think that it would be fairly obvious when we're triggered. Sometimes it is. Sometimes it comes on the scene with all the bells and whistles. Our muscles get tense, our heart rate quickens, and we feel restless, agitated, and on edge. But at other times, the experience can be very subtle. We might feel a slight sense of unease, a faint flicker of energy in our chest, or a quick, almost imperceptible twitch in our stomach. These sensations are distant echoes of past distress, sounding from somewhere in the deep recesses of our mind, body, and spirit. It's like when our alarm clock first goes off and we're still fast asleep. It comes to us softly at first, as if it's far away. The difference is that eventually the clock's buzzer breaks through and rouses us to attention; but anxiety signals, despite affecting our behavior, can fly under the wire and go unnoticed. Especially when we're not attuned to our physical experience.

In addition to being subtle, anxiety can show up in a number of unfamiliar and confusing ways. In fact, there may be times when we're feeling anxious, yet do not recognize it as such. In order to sharpen our senses and get better at detecting when anxiety is making an appearance, let's familiarize ourselves with the different possibilities.

Below is a list of anxiety-related responses. As you read over the different descriptions, check off any that seem familiar to you and might be a part of your emotional experience.

SIGNS OF ANXIETY

Muscle tension or constriction
(anywhere in your body)

Heart rate quickening

Restlessness, agitation

A desire to flee or withdraw

Shallow breathing, shortness of breath

Nausea, stomachache

Having to urinate

Confusion, difficulty focusing or thinking

Dizziness, lightheadedness, disorientation

Perspiring, cold hands/skin

Numbness, tingling, trembling, muscle twitches

As you can see, there's quite a range of ways in which anxiety shows up. However, most people find that their own experience, whatever it may be, tends to be fairly consistent. For instance, Sophie typically feels panicky and sick to her stomach when she's triggered. My experience is a little different. When a button gets pushed for me, I generally feel a kind of quivering sensation in my solar plexus, like a subtle electrical current quickly running down a wire. Sometimes it's so subtle that it could buzz right through me without my noticing it. In fact, I'm sure it was going on for quite a while before I caught on. But the more I've paid attention to my inner experience, the better I've gotten at noticing it.

With practice, the same can happen for you. To that end, let's do an exercise that will help sensitize you to your experience.

ANXIETY AWARENESS EXERCISE

Find a quiet place, free from distraction, where you can tune into what's going on inside of you. Get in a comfortable, relaxed position that allows you to be in full contact with the energy in your body. In general, sitting upright with your back straight and supported and your feet against the floor is best. Close your eyes and focus inward. Take a moment to allow yourself to settle. Take a few breaths and just observe your inhale and exhale without having to change anything.

Then think of a relationship scenario with your partner that would bring you to the edge of your emotional comfort zone. If you're not currently in a relationship, imagine being with a former partner or someone else from your life who is important to you. Picture a scenario that would require you to stretch outside of your usual way of being. For instance, you might imagine the prospect of openly sharing your sadness, disappointment, or hurt with a partner, letting your partner know that you're feeling insecure or afraid and need their reassurance or support, or telling your partner how much he or she means to you, how much you love and depend on them. Or you might picture directly addressing a conflict, telling your partner you're frustrated or angry about something they said or did and asking for what you would like to be different. You don't have to picture yourself following through on any of these things. Merely anticipating that you're about to do something that makes you anxious will likely be enough to get your nervous system to light up. That's all we want.

Visualize whatever situation you choose in as much detail as possible. Imagine yourself getting ready to open up and express yourself. As you lean into the experience, pay close attention to what's happening in your body—in your head, face, neck, shoulders, back, chest, in your arms, stomach, legs, everywhere. What happens inside of you as you anticipate being more open? Notice any areas of tightness, tingling, or discomfort. Notice where energy stops and where energy flows. Notice where you might feel warm and where you might feel cold. Just observe whatever you experience,

whatever happens for you, without having to
change it or do anything.

When you're done, take a deep breath, and let it go.
Shake off the experience. Feel it leave your body.
Feel yourself come back to center. Then take a
moment to write down the physical sensations
that you observed.

What was that like for you? What did you notice? Perhaps you discovered a few things about yourself and how you react. Maybe you noticed some physical sensations that you weren't aware of. If so, great! You're becoming more aware. On the other hand, maybe you didn't notice anything. Maybe it felt different or strange. That's okay, too. Every time you turn your attention inward, no matter what you find, you're growing your observation skills. You're expanding your awareness and strengthening your ability to attend. The more you do it, the better you'll get. Suddenly your efforts will pay off, and you'll notice something you hadn't seen before. Something that can be helpful to you.

Confession time. You know those pictures of astronauts walking on the Moon? All you can see is a little bit of rocky terrain and then everything drops off into an abyss of blackness? That's how it seemed to me when I first started to go inside and attend to my emotional experience. I felt like I'd landed on an unknown planet and all I could see was darkness. I'm not kidding. But over time, the more I turned my attention inward, the light of awareness began to dawn and I began to make contact.

And that's what you need to do: Tune into your felt experience repeatedly. Throughout your day, scan your body from head to toe and see what you notice. What do you feel? What sensations do you notice and where? Get into the habit of checking in with yourself especially when you're interacting with your partner. Doing so will build your awareness of, and connection to, your inner experience.

Then when you notice that you're feeling anxious, that you've gotten triggered, name it as such. Put a verbal label on it. You might say to yourself, "I'm triggered," or "I'm having a reaction," or "There goes my old wiring." Whatever phrase helps you note it and see it for what it is. Keep it short and sweet so that you don't get overly drawn into the experience and are able to keep it at a healthy distance. Naming when you're triggered will reduce your anxiety and make it easier for you to get unhooked.

You might also be able to identify what feelings, needs, and desires are coming up for you—the stuff at the bottom of the Triangle. Or maybe not. Getting to the core of your emotional experience will be the focus of the next chapter. At this step in your process, it's enough to know feelings are stirring in you that are making you uncomfortable. Some core way of being is daring to venture outside of your internal working models of how things "should" go in your relationship.

The "D" Corner of the Triangle

Short of recognizing when you're feeling anxious, the other sign that you're triggered is when you become defensive. As the stories of Karla, Craig, and Sheri from Chapter Two illustrate, the train has already left the station when we've reached this point, and our "fight-flight-or-freeze" response is up and running. We're already engaged in some kind of behavior whose sole purpose is to get us away from our discomfort.

In response to the fear and needs for reassurance that stir in Karla when she doesn't hear from Emily, she ruminates all day and then sulks at dinner. Craig recoils from Lydia's show of affection, blames her for being too needy, and withdraws in response to the underlying discomfort his own needs for connection evoke. Sheri reacts to the distress her needs for closeness and safety provoke by either attacking Rick, running from him, or doing a number on herself. All three are unaware that they've gotten triggered and are caught up in defensive patterns of behavior.

It can be hard for us to recognize when we're responding defensively. These behaviors can be so ingrained that they just seem to be an aspect of who we are, or part of our very nature. We don't realize what we're up to or that our reaction is actually a learned self-defense, a coping strategy that can be changed.

In general, the kinds of defenses that we resort to in our relationships tend to fall into two categories: hyperactivating or deactivating. Respectively, we're either turning up the volume on certain feelings (as in a temper tantrum like the one I described Sophie having earlier), or we're trying to make them go away (as when she questioned and doubted her feelings). In short, we're either "fighting," "fleeing," or "freezing." In any case we're avoiding expressing our core feelings, needs, or desires.

While each of us may respond to our feelings a bit differently, certain defense strategies seem to be more common than others. Becoming familiar with typical defenses will help you begin to recognize these sorts of behaviors in yourself.

Below is a list of some of the typical ways in which we respond to the sense of threat we experience when feelings arise in our relationships. We all behave in these ways from time to time, some more than others. As you read over the different descriptions, check off any that could possibly be ways in which you respond when you're triggered.

COMMON RELATIONAL DEFENSES

"Acting-out" our feelings rather than expressing them in a healthy manner (e.g., blaming, criticizing, making demands, having a temper tantrum)

Leading with one feeling over another (e.g., getting angry when we're actually feeling hurt or afraid, or becoming tearful or hopeless when underneath we're feeling angry)

Changing the subject, averting our eyes, or turning
away when feelings emerge

Talking rapidly, or so much, that our partner
can't get a word in edgewise

Not talking at all—going silent

Being dismissive of our own or our partner's
feelings; trying not to care

Withdrawing, detaching, shutting down

Self-criticism, blaming ourselves

Being passive-aggressive (i.e., expressing our
anger in passive ways such as not responding
to texts or phone calls, showing up late,
"forgetting" to do something)

Making excuses, justifying, or "rationalizing"
away our behavior

Distracting or busying ourselves, zoning out (e.g.,
checking our phone, surfing the internet, over
focusing on work, and the like)

Avoiding specifics, being vague, or denying how we
feel (e.g., "I'm fine." "Nothing's the matter.")

Any addictive behavior (e.g., alcohol, drugs, food,
sex, gambling, shopping, and such)

Intentionally pushing down or
suppressing our feelings

Do any of these defensive behaviors sound familiar to you? Might they be ways in which you respond when you're feeling anxious? Are there other things you do that might also serve a defensive purpose? Give it some thought.

It might help to make a list. Writing down our defenses can help us see them more objectively (as coping mechanisms) and recognize them more readily.

If you're having trouble recognizing when you're getting defensive, there are some telltale signs that can clue you into when you've gotten hooked. For instance, when the emotional tone of your experience suddenly shifts and goes from neutral to hot or cold; when your voice gets louder or tense, or quiet and fading away; or when your thinking and behavior become rigid or your reaction is out of proportion to whatever is happening.

These are all signs that you're in a "reactive state," responding with a sense of threat. Your perception has narrowed in on what's upsetting you, you're completely absorbed in your distress, and you can't see the forest for the trees. You're in self-defense mode and aren't receptive to others or able to see or hear them accurately. You've dug in your emotional heels and aren't about to budge. You're closed off.

In contrast, when you're in a "receptive state" you're open and flexible, able to hear your partner and consider different points of view. That doesn't mean you're not having feelings; you often are. But they're regulated, and you're able to stay connected and explore different ways of relating. When you're in an integrated, more balanced state, the thinking and feelings parts of your brain are working together. As Diana Fosha says, you're "feeling and dealing."[19]

Knowing the difference between how it feels to be in either a receptive or a reactive state can clue you into when you're triggered and being defensive. Here's a simple exercise developed by psychiatrist Daniel Siegel that can help you tell the difference.[20]

NO/YES EXERCISE

Find a quiet place where you are free to focus in on your felt experience. Settle in and feel yourself grounded. There's not a lot to this exercise. All you're going to do is say two words and notice how you feel. First, firmly and slightly harshly, say the word "no" out loud seven times. As you say it, notice what it feels like inside, how you feel in your body. Notice the energy, the sensations, the physical reactions. After you finish, pause and note what your experience is like. Okay. Take a breath and let it all go.

Next, in a kind and soothing tone, say the word "yes" seven times. As you do, notice again what your experience inside is, how it feels. After you finish, pause and note what you observed. Take a breath, and let it go.

Pretty striking difference, huh? "No" evokes the experience of how a reactive *fight-flight-or-freeze* state feels. Your muscles get tense, your walls go up, and you pull inward; you resist. When you're in this state, change and collaboration are practically impossible. Saying "yes," in contrast, relaxes your reactivity, you open up, and you are able to receive. It is here when the echoes of the past recede from your nervous system and you can come more fully into the present moment. The capacity to shift into and to be in this state is what you want to grow. When you are receptive, your best and most integrated self can show up. This is who you want to bring to your relationships.

So here's what you need to do: You need to put your observer hat on and pay attention to your behavior. As you interact with your partner, ask yourself: *Am I staying open or am I getting defensive? Am I revving up, or am I withdrawing or shutting down? Am I being reactive, or am I being receptive?* And when you recognize what's going on for you, name it as such (e.g., "I'm triggered," "I'm getting defensive," "I'm activated," and so forth).

Sometimes you won't realize that you're triggered and responding defensively until after the fact. That's okay. Better late than never! The fact that you're noticing it at all says that you're reflecting on your behavior and willing to learn about yourself. Nice! In the doing, you'll be more likely to recognize what's happening when it's happening. You're on your way to doing things differently.

So after an argument or a tense moment with your partner, spend some time reflecting on what just happened. Don't focus solely on what he or she did. Instead, let yourself also focus on your own behavior. Did you get defensive? If so, how? What did you do? What was happening for you? Get curious and see what you learn about yourself.

A COMPASSION BREAK

As you begin to observe yourself and discover what's been going on for you, how you've been responding, you may have some feelings. You may get down on yourself and think that there's something wrong with you. You may get upset that you haven't noticed these things before. That's understandable. But in these moments, I really want to encourage you to practice self-compassion. Just because you may get defensive at times doesn't mean there's something wrong with you. It just means you're human. You have a brain that can make you feel as though you are in danger when you're not and cause you to respond in predetermined ways. We all do. It can help to remember that this phenomenon is part of the human experience. As Kristin Neff, a pioneer in the study of self-compassion, points out, a fundamental element of self-compassion is recognizing that

you're not alone.[21] Many of us are struggling with
the same issues. We have nervous systems that were
shaped by our early experiences and developed
ways of coping that can be problematic at times.
We didn't get the kind of help we needed to do
things differently. We didn't get a manual to help
us navigate the world of our feelings in a healthy
way. We've just been doing the best we can. But
now you're learning what you need to know to
free yourself. That's what matters. That's what will
make the difference.

Then What?

Being able to recognize and name when you're triggered is a skill that
will improve the more you do it. And that's exactly what you need
to do. Practice being an emotion detective. Find any opportunity to
turn your gaze inward and observe your experience. When something
feels off, notice the different physical and emotional sensations you're
experiencing. Observe and get curious about the pull to respond in
a habitual way. Use the Triangle as your guide. Identify and name
what's happening for you.

When you get triggered, and you will—it's inevitable—try
to see it as an opportunity. Our anxiety and defenses are signposts.
They're telling us that we feel a need to express our true feelings,
needs, and desires. They're telling us that our core self is trying
to emerge. If we pause and give ourselves some room, we're then
afforded an opportunity to get to know ourselves more deeply.

You're probably wondering—*then what do I do?* This part can
be challenging and takes courage. Once you've noticed that you've
been triggered and have identified it as such, your task is to then do
nothing. That's right, nothing. Just allow your emotional experience
to be present and felt without responding or doing anything about
it. Drop your defenses and just be with what's inside of you. Easier

said than done, I know. When you've gotten triggered and resist responding as programmed, your amygdala gets a little bent out of shape. It still thinks that something bad is going to happen and goes into overdrive. It doesn't know any better, but you do, and that's what matters. It will eventually calm down, but in the meantime you have a serious choice to make. Do you want to strengthen old fear-based habits, or do you want to give yourself the opportunity to do something different?

By accepting and allowing for your emotional experience without responding to it as though you're in danger, you're interrupting the usual chain reaction and establishing a new way of being. You're draining the charge of reactivity from your implicit memory and bringing yourself into the present moment. You're changing your relationship to your felt experience and updating your brain wiring. You're freeing yourself up for something better.

CHAPTER TAKEAWAYS

- Mindfulness can help you more readily see and shift your emotional dynamics.

- Your amygdala can throw you into survival mode when it's not warranted.

- Observing and naming your experience can calm your nervous system and get you unhooked.

- Defenses, anxiety, and your core feelings are the main components of your emotional experience.

- The key to growing your emotional awareness lies in becoming more attuned to what's going on in your body.

- Anxiety and defenses are signs that you've been triggered and are in a reactive state.

- Being able to recognize and name when you're triggered is a skill that will improve the more you do it.

- Allowing your emotional experience to be present without responding or doing anything changes your brain's wiring.

CHAPTER FOUR

Step Two: Stop, Drop, and Stay

"Your vision will become clear only
when you look into your heart.
Who looks outside, dreams.
Who looks inside, awakes."

CARL GUSTAV JUNG

"This weekend was just brutal," Craig said, as he sat down, clearly in pain. He looked to me as though he'd been run over by a truck.

"What happened?" I asked with concern.

"Well, you know, Lydia and I were fighting. No surprise, I guess."

Craig, whom you originally met in Chapter Two, is an attorney in his early forties. He came to see me feeling distraught about his relationship with Lydia, his fiancée. Although they'd been together a while and engaged for over a year, he'd been unable tie the knot. His inability to move forward was taking a toll on both of them and was the source of much of the tension in their relationship. Craig was full of ambivalence—questioning his relationship with Lydia, doubting whether he could trust her, and worried that if they got married, it would just be a matter of time before it would all blow up in his face. Lydia, he feared, would turn on him and take him to the bank. Underneath it all, Craig was petrified.

From Craig's point of view, their weekend together had gotten off to a good start. They'd gone out with friends to celebrate Lydia's birthday and had a good time. But afterward, they'd no sooner gotten home than Lydia seemed to want more from him.

"I was like, 'Are you kidding me?'" Craig said to me, looking indignant. "We'd just spent a whole evening together. Man, I just can't win with her. No matter what I do." Craig continued on, telling me about the fight that ensued—the accusations, the blaming, the finger-pointing. An all too familiar pattern of their defenses leading the way that in the end got them nowhere and left them both feeling battle weary and wounded.

From what I knew about them, I suspected that Lydia was just being affectionate with Craig, wanting to connect with him once they'd gotten home. But given Craig's strong reaction, it was clear that something about that had triggered him and he was unable to see the moment objectively. After all, there are so many other ways he might have responded to her. Aside from possibly enjoying her embrace, if he really wanted some time to himself, he could have just told her that. Or if he was feeling criticized, as it seemed he was, he might have talked to her about it. But Craig was in a reactive state and not able to respond in a thoughtful way.

I felt sad. Craig was beside himself, at a loss about what to think, do, or feel, and ashamed of his inability to be successful in love as of yet. I knew how deeply he cared for Lydia and how awful he felt about hurting her, but his old wiring kept caging him in. Somewhere inside of him was a person longing to be close and connected but desperately afraid of taking the risk of opening up, desperately afraid of being hurt. If Craig was going to be able to rescue himself from his early programming and get somewhere better in this or any other relationship, he needed to get a better handle on what was going on inside of him.

As Craig talked, I could see that he was getting lost in the story, and it was time to change course and focus back on his feelings. "Craig, I can see how upsetting this is for you. I'm really sorry. You guys have been having a hard time. But instead of getting further into the details, I think it would be helpful to put the story aside and focus on what was going on for you emotionally. I might be wrong about this, but I think something about Lydia's trying to connect with you was triggering and put you on the defensive. Does that sound like a possibility?"

"So I screwed up?" Craig said, looking dismayed.

"No," I responded, empathically. "That's not what I'm saying nor how I see it. But I think your nervous system got the best of you. Let me share with you what I think is going on." I took out a sheet of paper, drew a Triangle on it, and mapped out Craig's emotional dynamics for him, explaining how his defenses were kicking in—going into "fight" mode—because he was feeling threatened. I pointed to the bottom corner, which I'd left blank, and asked Craig if he'd be willing to have a look at what core feelings might have gotten stirred up for him. That, I explained, would give us the best chance of turning this dynamic around. Looking slightly wary but willing, Craig agreed.

"Great," I said. "But first, let's take a minute or two to get grounded so that we can look at this from a more centered place. Move your feet a bit so that they're underneath you and take a moment to feel them against the floor. Feel your body supported by the couch. Just notice how you feel as you sit here with me." Craig sat up, shifted around a bit, settling in, and then looked at me for what to do next.

"Okay. Let's take a look at that moment with you and Lydia from the other night. But this time, let's see if you can put aside getting pissed. Let's try to slow things down a bit so we can see what else might be there. Okay?

Craig nodded.

"All right, go inside. Picture that moment and, as you do, just try to stay open to your experience. Just hang with it and let whatever happens happen."

Craig focused inward, sitting very still, his face intent and serious. Looking uncomfortable, he said, "Um, I feel kind of tense."

"Yeah. So something is making you anxious. That's usually why we tense up. Where in your body are you feeling tense? I asked, helping Craig to attune to and observe his felt experience.

"In my stomach."

"Can you describe what it's like? Describing it can help to ease some of the discomfort."

Craig put his hand on his stomach, sat with it for a moment, and then said, "I don't know. It kind of feels like pressure."

"Okay. You're doing great. Let's try and stay with that and give it a lot of room. Breathe into that place inside you and just notice what happens."

○   ○   ○

This is a pivotal moment for Craig. After nearly a lifetime of stuffing his feelings and soldiering onward, he's taking a risk and attempting to stay open. Instead of lashing out reflexively or shutting down, he's trying to stay present. Instead of turning away from his emotional experience, he's turning toward it and giving it some room. Not an easy task. It takes intention. It takes courage. The pull to do otherwise is so strong. But it's the only way to loosen the grip of his old programming. It's the only way to free himself from a fear that is no longer warranted.

Rewiring Your Emotional Circuitry

When we're triggered, our internal working models for feeling and dealing are activated. Our past emotional conditioning takes over, unconsciously distorting our perceptions and controlling our behaviors. But if we slow down our experience and stay present to our feelings, we're afforded a golden opportunity to disentangle ourselves from our early wiring.

When we're triggered, the activated emotions inside of us provide direct access into our implicit memory. If we can get curious and look at our feelings, if we stay open and listen to them, a picture begins to emerge in which the details of our early conditioning are laid bare, all those life experiences that got downloaded into our hardwiring and have been running the show become apparent. We can expose that which has been unconsciously controlling us. We can unpack it, rework it, and update it. We can heal the inner wounds that have long been festering. Ultimately, we can free ourselves from its spell and be transformed from the ground up.

In addition, when we stay present to our emotional experience, we discover that when fully felt, our feelings don't last forever, no matter how strong they may seem in the moment. Like an ocean wave, they grow in intensity, peak, and invariably dissipate. It's all the defensive maneuvering we unconsciously engage in that keeps them hanging around. When we suppress or distort our feelings, as we learned to do, they're not able to run their natural course. They get stuck and keep coming back to haunt us in some way, shape, or form. But by staying with our emotional experience, rather than being reactive, we can learn to move through it and get to a better place.

Over time, the more we stay present to our experience, our feelings become familiar, manageable, and less threatening to us. We come to see that they're not only *not* to be feared, but that they can actually be of great benefit to us. That's their purpose—to make our life better. Moreover, the more we lean into our emotional experience and see it through in its entirety, our amygdala softens its reactivity, and our neural programming gets updated. We come to have a friendlier response to our feelings, needs, and desires. Ultimately, we change the way we relate with ourselves, and in turn, how we can relate with others. In this way, learning to stay present with our feelings is an act of love.

Learning to abide with your emotional experience is the work of Step Two, "Stop, Drop, and Stay." [22] In this step, your main task is to put your defenses aside, focus inward, and stay present to what's going on inside of you.

When we're reactive and respond to our feelings by either shutting down or overreacting, it's a sign that our "window of tolerance"[23]—the zone of emotional arousal in which we're able to function most effectively—is constricted. There's not enough space in which the full extent of our emotional experience can comfortably reside. There's not enough room for the totality of our being, and so we're forced to play out a limited expression of ourselves.

I'm reminded of a Buddhism-inspired metaphor a colleague of mine, psychologist and mindfulness practitioner Miriam Marsolais, once shared when we were teaching a group of therapists together about how to help people abide with their emotional experience. It goes something like this: If you want to tame a wild horse, you need to give it a big corral. If you fence it in too tightly, the horse's energy will be destructive. But if the corral is wide and spacious, there's enough room for the horse to run, buck, snarl, and do whatever it needs to do to work out its pent-up energy. Eventually it settles down without causing any harm. It's not the horse's activation that's destructive. Rather, it's not having enough room within which to exist.

Our emotions need a wide, open corral as well.

When you stop, drop, and stay with your feelings, you expand the space inside of you so there's plenty of room for all aspects of your emotional experience to reside comfortably. The past, as it shows up in your nervous system, can coexist with our here and now self. What was once foreground, your emotional upset, can step back and be a part of a larger picture. As renowned Buddhist teacher Pema Chödrön aptly explains, "Peace isn't an experience free of challenges, free of rough and smooth, it's an experience that's expansive enough to include all that arises without feeling threatened."[24]

By dropping inside, you allow for a more integrated experience of yourself. You clear internal space so that your core self has room to emerge in its entirety. You can then relate with your partner from a more adult place, instead of one in which you're mired in the conditioning of your past.

As the name of this step implies, "stop, drop, and stay" consists of three different parts. Basically you're stopping the action, dropping inside yourself, and staying with your experience. It's a 1-2-3 sequence of smaller steps that in practice blends seamlessly into one broad movement. But for learning purposes, I'm going to break the sequence down and spend some time on each individual part so you can get a handle on what's entailed. Then we'll put them all together.

At this point in your process, the work of Step Two is meant to be done on your own instead of with your partner. You need time and space to get to know, explore, and work through your feelings before trying to do that while engaging with others. There may be unprocessed memories that need to be sorted through first. It's not that it can't be done while you're engaging with your partner; in fact, that's precisely what you'll eventually be doing. Later in the book, we're going to look at how to apply all of the four steps while we're relating with our partners.

But I really want you to take the time to get to know and sort through your own inner experience first. Give yourself a lot of room to practice being with yourself. The more you do, the easier it will become.

In a nutshell, "stop, drop, and stay" is all about engaging your attention in a new and constructive way. You start simply by stopping.

Stopping

"Stopping" is not about bringing our experience to a grinding halt or getting rid of any part of it. It's about stopping whatever we've been doing and slowing down so there's room to do something different. It's about interrupting our usual way of responding when we're triggered in order to move to Step Two—shifting our focus in a different direction. This aspect of Step Two overlaps with the tail end of Step One. You know, the place where you probably wanted to ask me—"and what the heck do I do now?!"

By stopping—recognizing and naming when you've been triggered—you've already begun to slow your process down.

However, as I'm guessing you've discovered in your learning process, your nervous system may still be giving you a run for your money. Although your finger is reaching for the proverbial pause button, the pull to go with the old familiar way of doing things is likely feeling tempting and strong.

Why is the pull so powerful? I mean, if we know that the old behavior is not helpful, why can't we just let it go? This is actually a telling question. Remember, the lessons that we learned during childhood about our feelings, needs, and desires? Our early conditioning occurred during a time when emotions were experienced as very intense. You were a child. You hadn't yet developed your ability to manage them. Thus, you experienced an extreme version of your feelings along with the intense fear that comes when your primary attachment relationships seem threatened. And as research shows, lessons learned during times of profound emotional experience are very strong and enduring. So the sense of threat that comes up for you around your emotions is intense because it comes from a very young place inside of you.

One way you can tell that this is the case is by looking at the beliefs imbedded in the fear you experience. If you ask the fear what it's afraid will happen should you let your defenses go, should you do things differently, the message you receive will likely be something like, "Everything will fall apart," "Someone will be destroyed," or "You'll be abandoned." If you step back and look at these beliefs, they don't make rational sense. That is, unless you're a child. When you were young, your thinking was not very nuanced. It was black and white, extreme, and full of absolutes. And your world was a very small place made up of just a few people. For a child, the possibility of losing connection feels catastrophic—it's a life or death matter. That's the fear that got entangled with your core emotional experience and now shows up in your adult life. That's why the pull to do something defensive to protect yourself is so strong. That's why letting go of the old way of doing things feels so threatening.

Recognizing and labeling your reactivity as old, as we did in Step One, can help to calm your distress, but sailing your emotional ship against the tide can still be challenging. What if you could further calm the sea and make it easier for you to move forward? That would certainly help. Here's where simple, practical tools for calming your nervous system can be so useful.

When you're activated, your *fight-flight-or-freeze* response is in gear, you're overcome by your distress, and that's all you can see. But if you can expand your awareness to include other aspects of your present moment experience, your perspective widens and becomes more balanced and realistic.

Mindfulness exercises in which you shift your focus to your here and now sensory experience can help you to see beyond your distress, connect with your surroundings, and feel more grounded. By intentionally focusing on a neutral aspect of your experience (for instance, whatever else you can see, hear, smell, and so on), you send a message to your amygdala that you're safe, and it's okay to put the brakes on. You relax the charge in your nervous system and free yourself up a bit so that you can do something different.

So at any time when you're feeling anxious or distressed, or you're having a hard time resisting the urge to respond defensively, try this:

GROUNDING TOOL

Shift your focus away from whatever is activating you and take a moment to notice what you're experiencing through any or all of your senses. Notice what you see, what you hear, what you touch, smell, or taste. For instance, notice how the chair you're sitting in feels against your body. Listen to the sounds of your environment and note what you hear. Look around the room and notice what you see. Notice what you smell in the air. Take a sip of a beverage and notice how it tastes. As you do these things, describe to yourself what you're

> observing. Let the experiences fully register. Feel
> yourself connect with them. Notice and appreciate
> what happens for you.

What happened as you tried to ground yourself? Did the energy inside you change at all? Are you feeling a little more settled and centered as a result? If so, great. If not, let's consider another option.

Focusing on your breath, a common practice in meditation, can also be calming.[25] In particular, when we breathe in a slow, measured way, the vagus nerve, the main channel of the parasympathetic nervous system, gets activated, and the nervous system as a whole comes into balance.[26] For that reason, any activity in which you regulate your breathing can be a powerful resource for calming yourself.

One breathing exercise that I like and use a lot with my clients employs what's referred to as "resistance breathing."[27] It involves using friction to slow the flow of air and slightly increase the pressure in our lungs, which in turn activates the calming part of our nervous system and slows us down.

Here's what you do:

BREATHING TOOL

Take a full breath through your nose and then, while pursing your lips as though you're letting air out through a straw, slowly exhale. Feel the air push against your lips as it slowly leaves your body. Do this three or four times, breathing in through your nose and out through the small opening in between your lips. As you do, you'll likely focus your attention on your breathing which will help to also shift your awareness. Notice what happens while

> you're breathing in this manner. You should feel
> the tension inside you begin to dissipate a bit. You
> should feel the edge softening.

Regulating your anxiety is especially important if you're someone whose feelings can get the best of you. You need to be able to calm the energy around them so that you can see your core emotions more clearly. On the other hand, you may have done such a good job of avoiding your feelings that when you do try to connect with them, you start to feel uncomfortable. That's actually a good sign as it means you're getting closer to your emotional experience. You're going to need to get used to feeling some degree of anxiety as part of your change process. In either case—feeling too much anxiety or not enough—your task is to find a way to lean into your emotional experience and work your growing edge in a way that feels manageable.

What I like about both of the tools I just shared with you, in addition to their calming effects, is that they can be done anywhere. You can practice them whenever you're feeling stressed (e.g., while you're driving in the car, waiting in line somewhere, in a work meeting) and have them ready for you when you get triggered. They're also pretty inconspicuous so you can use them without feeling self-conscious about being noticed. Experiment with both of them and figure out what works best for you.

Remember, though, that the point of doing either of these exercises is not to calm yourself so you can be on your merry way. We've got more work to do! You're simply trying to loosen up your distress just enough so that you can more easily shift your attention and be with your emotional experience from a more centered place— *stop* and then *drop*.

Dropping

"Dropping" is not about changing our physical position, as in getting down on the ground. Rather, it is about shifting our attention inward to a deeper place inside ourselves. It's about letting go of the storyline, getting out of the chatter in our heads, and connecting with what's going on in our bodies. It's about moving toward what's at the bottom of the Triangle: our core emotional experience.

To get a sense of what I mean, try this. Close your eyes for a moment and notice what happens when you do. As everything fades to black, notice how your inner experience suddenly becomes more apparent and feels nearer. Notice what's going on energetically for you. Notice what sensations you're experiencing in your body. Feel yourself "drop" into your experience.

Without visual distraction from the outside world, it's as if we take a step closer to our experience, as if we can inhabit ourselves more fully. This is exactly what you're striving for when you drop— to be more fully present with yourself. You're shifting your focus from looking externally to looking internally. As renowned couples therapist Sue Johnson suggests, you're taking your internal "elevator" down to the ground floor.[28]

In reality, you haven't moved anywhere. You're still in the same physical place whether your eyes are open or closed. Your shift in experience has to do with where you place your attention. You can focus outward, or you can focus inward. When you drop, you focus internally on what's going on inside of you. You move closer to your felt experience. This is what you need to do.

If it helps you to feel more in touch with your experience, you can close your eyes, but you don't have to. Simply by shifting your gaze from looking outward to one that is inwardly reflective can make a big difference.

In any case, once you drop inside yourself, your work now is to stay present. Instead of running from your emotional experience, you need to foster a new way of being with it. You need to accept it. You need to bring it into the light of awareness. You need to welcome and make room for it. You need to stay with it.

Staying

When we drop inside ourselves, we begin to approach that from which we had been running. We turn toward the emotions, needs, and desires that we've been conditioned to fear. The feelings deep inside us that we've attempted to disavow or hide. They've been trying to get our attention for a long time, but we didn't realize it. We've been too afraid to stay present and listen. We've been too distracted to notice that they're there.

When we're triggered our natural tendency is to avert our attention and move away from our discomfort. But when we do that, we're just perpetuating our distress. We're responding as though we're in danger, thus validating and reinforcing our threat response and never giving ourselves a chance to learn otherwise.

By staying with our emotions instead of reflexively exiting the scene, leaning into our discomfort and moving through it, we're challenging the fallacies of our early conditioning. We're calling its bluff and loosening the hold that fear has had on us and freeing ourselves from the past.

By staying with our emotional experience, abiding with it and giving it room to breathe, it's able to move through us and come to resolution. We come to see that everything will *not* come tumbling down, our relationships will *not* be ruined, our feelings *won't* destroy anyone, nor will we be destroyed. We come to see that ultimately we are better for it.

When you stay with your emotional experience and see it through, you grow your capacity to be present with yourself and with others. In doing so you develop a different kind of relationship with your emotional experience. Instead of responding to it as though it's the enemy, you befriend it. You give it a chance to be seen and heard, the same chance you'd give someone you care about who's feeling distressed. Someone who you want to relate to with kindness, patience, and respect. Don't you deserve the same?

When you're triggered, you need to become familiar with your experience. You need to get to know it. You need to meet it with open eyes and an open heart. When you do this, when you lean in and receive it with curiosity and a desire to understand, you are in a way re-parenting yourself. You're giving yourself the kind of sensitive attention you so desperately needed early on in life. The kind of care and support that would have helped you develop and flourish. The kind of caregiving that can enable you to do just that now.

How do you do that? Simply put, you stay with your experience and allow it to unfold.

Okay. I know. Easier said than done. It's hard to stay put when you feel uncomfortable, want to run, or feel confused. But you don't have to white knuckle your way through it (although it may initially feel that way). The key to growing your capacity to stay present with your experience lies in slowing it down and making it more manageable. As you know, you can use your breath to slow down your experience. And you can intentionally engage your prefrontal cortex by taking a participatory observational stance, one in which you both allow yourself to be with your experience while also observing it. You do this by paying attention to what's happening in your body—observing mindfully and describing to yourself your physical sensations—and noticing any images or beliefs that accompany your emotional experience. This practice of using your higher brain to manage your lower brain by simply observing the components of your emotional experience grows your affect tolerance—your ability to hang in there with strong emotions instead of being overwhelmed by them—and makes your emotions easier to be with. You notice them, name them, and watch them as you ride out the waves of your experience.

With this goal in mind, give this next exercise a try:

STAYING EXERCISE ONE

Close your eyes and go inside. Think about a recent relationship experience you've had in which you were triggered. Recall what happened. Picture it in your mind's eyes in as much detail as possible. As you do, notice what happens in your body. Find the place inside of you where you're feeling physically activated. Focus on it. Stay with it. Breathe into it and give it a lot of room. Allow yourself to feel whatever is there. Touch the quality of it. Describe it to yourself. Notice what happens as you do.

Let yourself get curious about what you're experiencing, not from an intellectual place of trying to make sense of things, but from a place of openness and discovery, allowing for whatever comes. Listen to whatever is there.

Try to look beyond your distress to see what feelings might be underneath. Ask yourself, "What's coming up for me?" Just notice what reveals itself. Notice how it manifests in your body. See if you can identify and name what emotions you feel (see pg. 103 side bar). Then just do your best to stay present and allow the feelings to move through you. Surf the waves of energy inside you. Feel them move through you. Stay with them as long as it takes for them to begin to shift.

If you start to feel overwhelmed, pause and focus on your breathing for a moment. Take a few deep breaths and let them out slowly. Use your breathing and grounding tools to help regulate your experience and make it more manageable. Do whatever you need to do to bring yourself back into your window of tolerance, where you're able to stay present to your felt experience without exiting in any way. Find a balance between leaning in enough so that you can be present with your feelings, but not so much so that you get ahead of yourself or feel overwhelmed.

If you're having trouble getting out of the story, putting your defenses to the side, you might wonder what you're afraid will happen if you do. Ask the fear, not your head, what it anticipates. Remember, your defenses developed to protect you. So try asking the fear what it's protecting you from. Listen for the answer. Ask yourself what you might feel if you were to let go of your defenses. What might you do? What might you say? What might happen? Notice any resistance or tension in your body and breathe into it. Try to soften it and let it go.

Then come back to your emotional experience and give it another try. Picture the triggering moment and notice what comes up for you now. If it's helpful, you can alternate between focusing on your breath (or some other neutral point of focus) and touching back into your emotional experience. Keep coming back to your emotional experience and staying with it until it shifts.

What was that like? What did you experience? Were you able to stay present with yourself. Was it as difficult as you anticipated? Did it help to observe and describe your emotional experience? Were you able to identify what you were feeling? What did you learn about your inner experience? Did you discover any feelings you weren't aware of?

There is no right or wrong answer to any of these questions. There's only your experience. What matters most is that you're trying to stay present to yourself. You're stretching and expanding your emotional capacity. You're widening your corral. In the doing, your emotional experience will become clearer over time.

If you noticed yourself getting distracted by your thoughts, judging yourself, or moving away, that's okay. It's hard to stay with your discomfort, especially when your old programming is telling you to do otherwise. Your defenses are ever ready to jump in and do their old song and dance routine. But what matters more here is that you're noticing that you're inclined to move away. You're becoming mindful of your process, of what's happening for you, instead of mindlessly going along for a ride.

WHAT AM I FEELING?

While there are many words used to describe how we feel, in actuality there are only a few core emotions. Everything else is a variation on a theme. Our main feelings are anger, sadness, fear, joy, interest (which includes love), surprise, shame, and disgust. Although any emotion can be troubling for us, the ones that we most often have a difficult time with in our relationships are fear, sadness, shame, and anger along with their related needs for safety, security, comfort, reassurance, understanding, empathy, support, respect, and the like. In addition, some of us learned to suppress our natural vitality so feelings like joy and love, along with their related needs for appreciation, delight, acceptance, and connection, can cause us conflict as well.

Moments such as these are revealing. You get to see in real time how you've been unconsciously responding to your emotional experience. You get to see what you've been doing all along but didn't realize until now. When you notice what's happening, you're no longer in the dark. You're keeping the light of awareness on and catching yourself. In these moments, you can say with a sense of wonder and discovery, "Wow. Look at that! Look at what just happened! Look at how my brain's conditioned!" You can note the impulse to escape the present moment, and then bring yourself back to your here and now. Every time you catch yourself and come back to your felt experience, you're strengthening your capacity to stay. This is the essence of practicing mindfulness.

You're going to feel some anxiety and distress. That's to be expected, especially if you typically withdraw from your feelings. You're taking a risk and doing something different. You're opening the closet door and turning on the lights to see if there's actually a monster hiding inside.

While it may seem counterintuitive, leaning into your distress rather than pulling away from it can actually help to decrease it. Resistance is what perpetuates your discomfort. But if you lean in and give it your attention, it starts to open up and shift. As you do, the knot inside you begins to unwind and the varied strands of your experience reveal themselves.

O   O   O

More than Meets the Eye

Craig took a breath and focused back inside on the pressure he was feeling in his stomach. He sat very still with his hand on his belly, doing his best to stay present. Then all of a sudden he seemed to shudder. His shoulders tensed up as he quickly turned his head to the side. It was as though he'd seen something upsetting, something that was painful to look at, something he'd rather not see.

"What is it Craig?" I asked. "What did you notice?"

"Um. I . . . I . . . wow, this is really strange. I don't . . . I don't know why I'm having this memory," Craig said.

"Oh, that's so important. I'm sure it's relevant. What did you see?"

"Um, I don't know. I must have been like five or six-years-old. It's nighttime. I'm in my bed alone. I feel sick to my stomach. I don't know why. Probably stress. I mean, my parents had just gotten divorced and my father was being such a jerk. Anyway, I was lying there in the dark and I wanted to call for my mother, like I wanted her comfort, you know?"

"Of course you did," I responded, feeling for him.

"But I just . . . I just didn't want to bother her. My poor mother, she was under so much pressure raising us on her own. I didn't want to add to it. I didn't want to give her any more problems. She had it tough enough. But . . . it was scary."

"So scary," I said, again pained by Craig's story. "You were a little boy. You needed someone to take care of you and be with you to help you deal with everything you were going through. We all need that."

"So . . . I remember like trying to compress my stomach and seeing if I could make the pain go away, kind of like doing sit-ups. And that's what I'd do. I would tighten my stomach and make the pain go away."

"Craig, that's so sad to me that you were all alone when you needed love and care, that you felt you had to make your feelings go away."

Craig looked at me with pain in his eyes as tears began rolling down his cheeks.

○   ○   ○

Getting to the Source

As Craig is discovering, when we stay with what's been triggered inside of us, it very often leads us to its source—the attachment injuries where the feelings and beliefs we are experiencing in the present originated. It's as though our emotions open up a portal through which we can see into our past. By staying and remaining open to what's going on inside of us, the emotional experiences that provide the foundation for our internal working models reveal themselves. The fog begins to clear, and potent memories come into view.

I've seen this happen so many times with my clients as we explore their emotional experience when they've been triggered. Invariably, they're taken by surprise when a memory arises, seemingly out of nowhere and totally unbidden. While it may seem as though that's the case, it's not. The memories that come up for them are what cause them to be triggered in the first place. They're the emotional lessons they learned that have been informing their amygdala's response. Together, we're able to draw a line from their reactivity all the way back to those early experiences and conversely trace it back in the other direction. The feelings and beliefs they're having in the here and now are echoes of what they experienced in the there and then.

But in general, we're not accustomed to looking below the surface. We just focus on whatever it was that triggered us. We focus on the person in front of us instead of looking inside ourselves. We don't realize our past has infiltrated the present and is coloring everything we see and do. But when we drop inside and stay with our experience, we come face to face with the memories that are fueling our reactivity and informing our behavior. In this way, our triggered state is, to borrow a phrase of Freud's, a "royal road to the unconscious."

As Craig stays with his feelings, the underpinnings of his abrupt response to Lydia begin to emerge. Tracing his reactive state back in time we discover a boy afraid of needing anyone. A boy rocked by his parents' divorce, his father's absence, and callous behavior. A boy afraid of his fragile world falling apart. In a heartbeat, his father was gone. Could the same thing happen with his mother? Lying in his bed alone, longing for his mother's love and care but afraid of doing anything that might unduly burden her, what was he to do? To his child mind, his attachment needs were potentially dangerous and as far as he could tell would only bring him disappointment and pain. His strategy was to make them go away, stuff his feelings, needs, and desires down and go it alone. He figured out a way to deal so as not to feel.

Now many years later, Craig's nervous system is still governed by the same unwritten rules. When the prospect of closeness with Lydia presents itself, he reacts as though he's in danger. His implicit memories remind him of those potent early lessons. It's as if there's a little boy inside warning him not to need anyone—*don't let yourself get too close, you'll be hurt!* In response, and without thinking, Craig springs into fight mode, effectively pushing Lydia away, protecting himself, or the child within him, from danger.

But when Craig goes inside and stays with his experience, implicitly stored memories bubble up into his conscious awareness. He sees and makes contact with the boy inside of him. The child still lying in his bed trying to make his feelings go away. He begins to bear witness to the longing, fear, and pain he felt as a child, the feelings inside of him that had nowhere to go, the feelings he learned to suppress and avoid. As he stays present to his experience, the unprocessed feelings of the past begin to release and move through him.

When we're triggered, it's as though a young part of us has been activated; the child who learned to fear his feelings, needs, and desires; our child self, stuck in time, still holding all the feelings that needed to be felt, still hoping that someone will come to the rescue and free him from the bind he is in.

In order to calm the emotional storm inside of us, we need to attend to the source of our triggering. We need to go to the place where the damage was done. We need to find the child inside of us still trapped by these early lessons, still carrying the burden of unprocessed feelings, unmet needs, and desires, and set him or her free.

Now I'm guessing that you're either resonating with this idea that there's a stuck child inside you, or you may be rolling your eyes. If this concept makes sense to you, sit tight for a moment. If it strikes you as strange or silly, I get it. I had a similar response many years ago when I heard counselor and self-help guru John Bradshaw talk about "healing the child within" on one of his PBS television shows. I had appreciated so much of what he talked about in the program but just couldn't relate to this idea that there was a wounded child in me that needed attention. At the time it seemed hokey to me and made me uncomfortable (that in itself should have been a sign).

Years later in therapy as I began to open up to my emotional experience, I came to understand viscerally what Bradshaw was trying to say. I discovered inside of me feelings from my past that had long been held in limbo, feelings that were just waiting to be heard, seen, honored, and find a way out. They were all the feelings I wasn't able to manage or work through at the time that they were evoked; all the pain, loneliness, and fear that I felt as a child that had gone unwitnessed and uncared for; all the anger that felt too dangerous to feel. It was as if my child self was finally given the permission to have his feelings.

As I allowed myself to feel and work through my feelings by sharing them with my caring therapist, my internal experience began to shift. I discovered a sense of compassion for my younger self for all he'd gone through, and I wanted to be there for him and attend to his feelings; to calm his fear, honor his anger, and empathize with his pain and shame. And as I did, the past receded to its rightful place. I felt myself come more fully into my adult self.

The truth is that when emotional experiences are suppressed, when they're not processed through to completion as they need to be, they stay stuck inside of us and don't go away. That's why we get triggered. They're still alive in our memories with all of the emotional charge of the past, all the potent feelings, beliefs, perceptions, and expectations that overtake our present moment when we're triggered.

Although much emotional healing can occur in the context of a loving, adult relationship, some memories and their inherent feelings and beliefs can stay locked away behind our defenses. As such, they don't receive the attention, love, and care our partner or other people in our lives may offer us. They remain sealed off from and unaltered by the disconfirming experiences we may be having; the experiences that tell us that we *are* worthwhile, that we *are* loved and cared for; the things we "know" but may not be able to fully feel.

For instance, a part of Craig is still afraid of trusting Lydia. Even though he may have all the evidence in the world that she is a good person, inside he still suspects that it's dangerous to open his heart and allow anyone close.

But don't get hung up on the idea of an actual child inside of us. It's just a concept. There are stuck emotional states stored in our implicit memory that get activated when we're triggered and need to be addressed.

Certain memories can remain cordoned off from our life experience unless we find a way to soften our defenses so that the healing light of the present can get through and undo the darkness and pain inside of us. We need to find a way to open the door to our past so that we can drain it of its emotional charge and put it to rest. We can do that by attending to the child within us.

Seeing your suffering as though it is coming from a child-self can make it easier for you to stay with and attend to these emotional states when they arise. Instead of being overly identified with the emotions that get activated in you when you're triggered, you can observe them and begin to relate to them as though they're coming from a part of yourself, not from the whole. In turn, you can disentangle your past from your present (your child-self from your adult-self) more readily. In addition, by understanding that your distress comes from a young place inside of you, you can more easily approach it with compassion and kindness instead of the frustration and defensiveness we all have a tendency to feel toward our adult-selves.

Getting triggered is actually a gift. A wounded part of you is sending up a flare so that you can find him or her. If you can find the child within you, so to speak, you can take care of him or her. You can be there for this child, you can attend to its feelings, you can relieve its suffering. By staying with your emotional experience, you can uncover the root of your struggle. Your discomfort is another important signpost on your emotional journey, pointing you down a path that can lead you to your emotional freedom.

When you stay with your emotional experience and open your heart to the unprocessed feelings inside you, you can release the pent-up energy that's been activating your nervous system. You can begin to deactivate the explosives in the minefield of your implicit memory that have been causing you to get triggered.

STAYING EXERCISE TWO

Recall a recent relationship experience that was triggering and still feels somewhat charged to you when you think about it. You might return to the experience you used in the previous exercise or work with something else. Get a mental image of what happened that was distressing for you. Then close your eyes and go inside; locate where you're feeling activated in your body.

Focus on your physical experience and give it a lot of room. Notice what happens when you do. Feel into your emotional experience. See if you can identify and name what you're feeling. Are there any images that come with the feelings? Are there any thoughts that arise? Do you notice any negative beliefs (for instance, "I'm a bad person," "I'm in trouble," "I can't trust anyone," "I'll be hurt," and such)? Just stay open to your experience and see what arises.

Then while focusing on your felt experience along with whatever images and beliefs arose, trace the whole experience back in time. Not intellectually. You're not trying to figure it out with your head. Just let your mind open up and follow the constellation of feelings, images, and beliefs as far back as it goes. As you do, notice whatever comes into your awareness. You might ask yourself, where is this coming from? How far back does it go? How young does it feel? And then see what comes.

Look deeply into the core of your emotional experience and see what you discover. Can you locate it in time? Can you see the child who has

been holding all these feelings? What's going on for
him or her? What is she contending with? What is
making him feel afraid, sad, vulnerable, or unloved?
What's causing her to feel ashamed, angry, or
upset? How do you feel as you see and witness this
child's experience, as you honor his or her feelings?

Notice what happens for you emotionally. Stay
open to whatever comes. Let yourself feel. Let
the child inside you feel. Give the feelings a lot
of room to be felt, to move through you, to be
processed. Stay with it as long as you can and as
long as it needs. Take some time to reflect on what
came up for you, what you experienced, what you
discovered, and what you learned.

Taking Care of (or Parenting) Yourself

When you stay with your emotional experience, giving it breathing
room to move and flow through you, you're attending to your
original pain. You're allowing stuck memories or emotional states to
process through to completion and lose their charge. You're allowing
the child inside of you to have its feelings and be witnessed and held
in the process. As psychologist Richard Schwartz explains, we're
"unburdening" our younger selves from the extreme feelings and
beliefs that they've been carrying.[29] In short, we're healing ourselves.

Sometimes that may be all you need to do. Sometimes dropping
inside and allowing yourself to feel what's there is enough to calm and
heal the source of your distress. It enables you to begin to disentangle
yourself from the past and see your present reality more clearly. But
sometimes what's inside of you is stubborn and holds on. Sometimes
it needs more attention. When this happens, you may need to figure
out what the stuck child inside of you needs in order to be freed from

the bind it's in. Then you can use your imagination to help him or her get those needs met.

Let's come back to Craig so you can see what this process might be like. Looking back at the memory that arose for him, Craig would see that his child-self, lying in bed distressed, needed to be comforted, held, and supported. He needed to know that he was loved and would be taken care of. With that in mind, Craig might then imagine going to his child-self, sitting down next to him, and taking his hand. He might let the boy know that he sees his distress, understands his fear, and empathizes with all that he's been going through. He might rub the child's back or take him in his arms as he tells him how much he is loved, how all of his feelings are okay and that he doesn't need to hide or be ashamed of them, and that he's not a burden. Craig might picture himself lying down next to the boy and holding him until he falls asleep.

Now you might be thinking to yourself that imagining such a scenario is not real and won't make a difference. Well, it's true that it's not real, but it can make a difference. As research shows, when you picture doing something with intention, your brain is activated in the same way as it would be if you were actually carrying out the behavior.[30] The same neurons start firing and wiring together, laying down new neural networks. Thus, imagination has the power to change the structure of your brain. By imagining healing scenarios in which your early emotional needs were met, you can create new, attachment-based, internal working models and update your programming. That's nothing to balk at.

But there is a qualifier when it comes to imaginal work. The experience needs to be felt. You need to engage in this process on an emotional level. You see, implicit memories are stored on the right side of the brain. If you're going to open them up and work them through, you need to utilize right-brain processes. It can't be done through logic or reason. It needs to be infused with emotion, and the experience needs to be embodied. It needs to be felt. That's what makes the difference. Remember, new emotionally rich experiences are what change us.

With that in mind, give this next exercise a try.

IMAGINAL CAREGIVING EXERCISE

Recall a relationship experience that was triggering and still feels charged to you. You might return to the experience you used in the previous exercise or work with something different. Get a mental image of what happened that was distressing for you, then close your eyes and go inside. Locate where you're feeling activated in your body.

Follow your feelings back in time to the hurt, scared, angry, or distressed child inside of you. Through your adult eyes, look at the child in your memory. If you have a hard time visualizing, don't worry about it. Just imagine the following in whatever way that works for you. All that matters is that you engage emotionally and that you have a felt experience.

Ask yourself, *what does this child need? What would have made this situation better for it?* Perhaps it just needs someone there to hold its hand. Maybe it needs someone to recognize, validate, and empathize with its pain, sadness, or anger. To hear it out. To tell it that it's loved, is good enough just the way it is, that everything will be okay. Maybe it needs to be taken somewhere where it will feel safe, to know that it's protected. Maybe it just needs to be held. Listen to your heart. Let it guide you. Deep inside you know what your child-self needs. You know what will make things right.

When you get a sense of what your child-self
needs to be unburdened, picture your adult-self
caring for it in just the right way. Picture your
adult-self really giving the child the care that he
or she needed. Help the child feel what it's like to
be seen, heard, to be cared for and loved. Give
your child-self whatever he or she needs from
you. Let yourself feel what it's like for the child.
Let yourself feel what it's like to be met in this
way. Let yourself feel, as an adult, what it's like
to be there for the child. Let all the feelings flow.
Let your experience be deeply felt. Stay with the
feelings as long as they need.

If you find it challenging to direct feelings toward
your younger self, try imagining how you might
respond if the child in your memories was someone
other than yourself. Perhaps you have children
of your own or have siblings or friends who have
children. Imagine how you'd feel toward him or
her if they were suffering in kind. Notice how that
makes you feel inside. Let yourself be with those
feelings, let them deepen. Then imagine directing
those feelings toward your younger self.

Similarly, if you find it difficult to imagine your
adult self being there for the child, imagine
someone else instead. Picture an ideal parent,
real or imagined, someone who has just the right
qualities to meet the child's needs. Someone who is
able to really be there for your child self.

What was that like for you? Were you able to imagine being
there for your younger self? If you were, how did that feel? Did it make
a difference in your experience? Did it change how you feel inside?

Maybe you found it difficult to imagine engaging in the kind of caring that would have met your early needs. Maybe you found it hard to feel for your younger self. That's actually not uncommon. Many people struggle with being able to feel compassion for their younger self. For that matter, many people struggle with feeling compassion for their adult selves as well. The sad truth is, if we weren't cared for as children in ways that were sensitive and attuned, if we didn't feel valued, respected, and loved, it's hard for us to respond to ourselves in a caring way. We have no frame of reference to draw on, no internal working model for what self-compassion looks like. We lack an inner voice that tells us we're okay, that we'll be okay, that we're worthwhile and lovable, and that we're not alone. In short, it's hard to imagine being this way if we've not experienced it. If we had, it would be an available internal resource for us, there for the taking.

In addition, our defenses can impede our attempts. We turn to look at our child-self and feel nothing, or worse we feel frustration, disgust, or contempt. Why, you may wonder? Well, some of us adapted to our early experiences in life by learning to blame or give ourselves and our feelings a hard time. As children we presumed or got the message that it was our fault if things weren't going well with our caregivers, if we were not being attended to, or if we were treated poorly. So we figured that if we can get control over ourselves, if we can whip ourselves into shape, then things will be better with our parents. Things will change.

If this is true for you, perhaps you imagined and hoped that they'd treat you differently, that they'd be there for you in the ways you needed, that they'd love you. Maybe such a strategy worked to some degree. And maybe it helped you feel a modicum of security. Maybe it kept you from being overwhelmed by feelings of pain and sadness.

Trouble is, the strategy was likely built on a false assumption. It wasn't your fault that your parents couldn't meet your needs or treated you poorly. You weren't responsible for their behavior. You were a child. Yet like other coping strategies that you developed early in life, it may persist. You may continue to be hard on yourself. You may continue to feel bad about yourself. You may continue to criticize and blame yourself. If that's the case, no wonder it can be challenging to feel some self-compassion.

But that doesn't mean you can't develop it. After all, it's innate to feel empathy and compassion. You were born with the capacity to do so. It's what enables you to connect with others. You just have to loosen up your defenses a bit, find it inside of yourself, and cultivate it. And you need to allow yourself to receive it.

If you're having trouble feeling for your younger self, if you're getting stuck in negativity, try this:

NEGATIVE BELIEFS EXERCISE

Think of the negative beliefs that come up for you about yourself. All the things you think about or say to yourself ("I'm a loser," "It's all my fault," "I can't do anything right"). Write them down on a piece of paper. Then picture a child you know, one who you care about, and imagine saying those things to him or her ("You're a loser," "It's all your fault," "You can't do anything right"). Give it a shot. Read down the list of statements out loud as if you're saying them to a child.

What is that like? What does it feel like to say these things? How do you imagine the child feels hearing them? Chances are it's hard for you to even bring yourself to say them to a child. Maybe you weren't able to. That's understandable. It feels so harsh and unfair. Nevertheless, that's how you've been treating yourself. That's how you've been treating the child inside of you. Take a moment to let that realization sink in. Notice how it feels. Then ask yourself if that's what your inner child needs to heal and grow. I'm guessing the answer is no. So consider what

kind of parent can help this stuck part of you heal.
Isn't that who you'd rather be?

Practice, Practice, Practice

We covered a lot of ground in this chapter. My intention was to give you a broad framework within which you can utilize the different tools I shared with you depending on what's needed. Not all of what we've covered here is required every time we *stop, drop, and stay*. Sometimes it's enough just to notice what's happening inside of us and make a little room for it in order to be able to separate ourselves out from what's been triggered. Merely seeing what's been activated inside of us can free us up enough to be able to engage with our partners in a healthier way. But at other times, we have more work to do. The knot inside of us is tightly wound and it takes time and effort to be unraveled.

Our capacity to stay with our emotional experience doesn't grow overnight. After all, think about what we're trying to do. We're challenging the status quo. We're forging new ground. We're learning how to attend to our inner experience mindfully. We're cultivating an altogether different way of being with ourselves. Naturally it's going to take some time.

But every day we're given plenty of chances to practice staying. To push the pause button, slow things down, and be with our internal experience. To get to know what's happening inside of us. To work with our experience and sort it out before we respond. If we pay attention, we get ample opportunity to practice, and that's what it takes. As the saying goes, "practice, practice, practice."

Our primary goal at this point in our process is to be able to calm the activation inside of ourselves when we're triggered so we can see what's going on for us more clearly; so we can have choices; so we bring a more mindful self to our relationships. Our long-term goals are to continue to grow our skills, attend to and heal our inner wounds, and to free ourselves from our past conditioning.

We don't have to be completely healed to have better relationships. That's not realistic. But when we can be with our emotional experience and effectively respond to different aspects of it, we can bring our better self to our relationships and relate to our partners more skillfully. We can speak to them from our adult-self, rather than through the eyes of an overwhelmed, frightened child.

○   ○   ○

In fact, this is precisely what Craig did. With a better understanding of what was going on for him, Craig took a risk and tried something different. When he got home from his therapy session, he could tell Lydia was still smarting from their recent upheaval. In the past Craig would have kept his distance and waited things out, hoping it would eventually blow over. Instead, he tried talking with Lydia. He told her about what he'd discovered in our work together. What he was learning about himself. How he lashes out when he's afraid. He shared some of his history with Lydia and explained why it hasn't felt safe for him to be vulnerable with her.

An amazing thing happened. Lydia softened. She thanked him for being open, empathized with him, and told him she understood. The tension between them, which could have gone on for days, subsided. Craig told me that it was such a relief and that it felt good to connect in this way. He actually felt closer to Lydia.

While there was still more work for Craig to do, he was beginning to turn things around. He was freeing himself from the past and developing a new, healthier way of relating. One that held the promise of something much greater for him and Lydia.

CHAPTER TAKEAWAYS

- When we're triggered, the activated emotions inside of us provide direct access into our implicit memory.

- The more we stay present to our emotional experience, the more our feelings become familiar, manageable, and less threatening to us.

- When we stop, drop, and stay with our feelings, we expand the space inside of us so there's room for all aspects of our emotional experience to comfortably reside.

- Shifting our focus to a neutral aspect of our here and now experience and slowing our breathing can help regulate our emotional experience.

- Leaning into our distress rather than pulling away from it can help to decrease it.

- When emotional experiences are suppressed and left unprocessed, they don't go away and cause us to be triggered.

- Staying present to our emotional experience allows stuck memories or emotional states to process through to completion and lose their charge.

- Imagining healing scenarios in which our early emotional needs are met can relieve us of our original pain and create new neural circuitry to support healthier relating.

CHAPTER FIVE

Step Three: Pause and Reflect

"Human freedom involves our capacity to pause, to choose the one response toward which we wish to throw our weight."

ROLLO MAY

Paula decided to take a walk on her lunch break for a change. Maybe the fresh air would help clear her mind. She'd been on an emotional rollercoaster all morning—at one moment feeling irritated with her husband Ivan, and then questioning herself, feeling anxious and worried the next. She kept thinking about the conversation they'd had the night before. Well, it wasn't exactly a conversation.

Paula had wanted to talk with Ivan about feeling disconnected from him. He'd been so consumed with his work lately that they hardly had any time together, and when they did he was distracted or too exhausted to do anything. She'd been feeling lonely in their relationship and hoped to connect with him and get back on track. But when they finally had a moment to talk, the conversation took a predictable turn, with Ivan launching into a monologue about how stressed he'd been with work and questioning why Paula didn't seem to understand and was putting so much pressure on him.

Paula got a sinking feeling as she listened to him. She'd been down this road before. Whenever she tried to get through to Ivan about his work schedule and making more time for the two of them, he'd get defensive. Somehow it would get all twisted around and end up with Paula feeling guilty and apologizing for being insensitive or unreasonable.

The more Ivan talked the more frustrated Paula grew. She wanted to blurt out, "This isn't about you! It's about me! It's about us! Can't you get that?" But as she was about to voice her anger, she felt a familiar wave of anxiety come over her and stop her in her tracks. She felt afraid. Afraid of going too far. Afraid of what might happen. And then the doubts crept in. Maybe she *was* being unfair? Maybe she *was* expecting too much? *He's doing the best he can,* she thought, trying to convince herself.

Ivan didn't seem to notice Paula's eyes begin to glaze over, nor did he sense the flame that was burning somewhere deep inside her. For that matter, neither did Paula. Not really.

Paula stepped outside, walked across the street to the park by her office, and sat down at a picnic table. She took a sandwich out of her lunch bag, started to unwrap it, and then put it down. She felt too unsettled to eat. She turned to look at the trees in the distance and thought again about Ivan. *I'm always there for him. Why aren't my needs important? Why can't he put his work aside once in a while and make time for us?* Her face grew warm and her jaw tightened as she thought to herself, *Is that so much to ask?*

Feeling a sense of certainty and a flash of determination, Paula vowed that she'd try to set the record straight with Ivan when she got home from work that night, and this time hold her ground. But when she pictured his face and imagined asserting herself, her chest tightened. The sense of strength she felt just a moment ago seemed to dissolve into nothing. In an instant, she felt like a little girl, afraid that something horrible might happen if she asserted herself. *Why is this so scary for me?* Paula wondered as she closed her eyes, trying to stay present with her fear, to face it down and not let it get the best of her. Then to her surprise an image of her mother's scowling face came into view. The answer suddenly became clear to her.

○ ○ ○

A Ghost from Childhood's Past

Paula's old wiring gets triggered in her experience with Ivan. What seems to her like insensitivity and self-involvement on his behalf incites her anger, and with that, her early conditioning kicks in. The threat alarm goes off to tell her that she's in danger, and she responds accordingly, battening down the emotional hatches and dutifully waiting for the storm to pass. Her old internal working model reminds her that healthy anger will be met with disapproval and disdain, and Paula shoves her feelings down just as her younger self had to do to maintain a safe connection with her mother.

Had Paula recognized what was happening, that the sense of threat that she experienced was based on the past and had nothing to do with the present moment, and had she given herself some room to explore her reaction, the tangle inside of her might have had a chance to unwind. She might have freed herself up a bit from the grip of fear and found the courage to try a different response. Instead she reacted mindlessly and followed the dictates of her now outdated internal working models. But as is often the case when we're triggered, the buzz in her nervous system persisted as her core self itched to make itself known. The old way of doing things was not sitting right with her anymore. Something needed to change.

Finally, a curtain parted to reveal what's been going on behind the scenes. A questioning and then an inward glance exposed the underpinnings of her distress, the origins of a fear that kept her from expressing her needs, that dissuaded her from acting on her behalf lest she risk destroying her most important relationship. At least that's what her nervous system anticipated.

In a matter of seconds, the missing pieces of a puzzle were laid before her, essential clues that could help Paula unravel the mystery of her struggle and allow her to get to a better place. Will they register for her? Will she put them together in a way that enables her to begin to leave the past behind and bring a more balanced and integrated self to her present moment experience? Or will they become a passing thought and disappear in a cloud of anxiety and distress?

Insight and Beyond

In Step Two, our focus was primarily on making room for our emotional experience. We put thinking aside and worked to stay present with our feelings—allowing for them, attending to them, and moving through them. We went on an experiential journey that helped us reconnect with estranged aspects of ourselves—the feelings, needs, and desires that had been omitted by our early attachment programming. So what do we do now?

Having reached a clearing in the forest of our feelings, we need to take time to reflect on our experience and make sense of what we discovered. We need to step back, survey the landscape, and consider what we've learned about our emotional dynamics. We need to take the time to understand our emotional experience, appreciate its impact on us, and listen to what it's telling us. And we need to figure out how best to respond to our partners to move forward in our relationships.

This is the work of Step Three, "Pause and Reflect," where self-reflection—examining, contemplating, and appreciating your experience—is the fuel that will power your continued healing and growth. This kind of self-reflection and deep-seated understanding is very different from the thinking that we worked hard to put to the side in Step Two, as what follows below makes very clear.

As you know, insight alone doesn't get many of us very far. We can understand all too well why we do some of the problematic things we do, but that doesn't necessarily make it any easier for us to not do them and change our behavior. This is why I've been so focused on the importance of being with your emotional experience. I want to help you make changes from the ground up—changes that are rooted in your emotional truth and will deepen and strengthen over time.

But experience without understanding can have limited benefits. After all, how does any of us know we've had an experience, let alone learn from it, if we don't pause and take time to reflect on it?

Reflecting on our experience has numerous benefits. By stepping back and looking at what got activated inside of us and thoughtfully considering what we've discovered, that reflection helps us reintegrate core feelings, needs, and desires back into our emotional repertoire, back in other words into our sense of self. We come to see more precisely how the internal working models of our past have controlled our present relationship experience and constricted our range of options. We're better able to recognize emotionally vulnerable spots inside us that make us susceptible to getting triggered. Then we come to understand more clearly what's been thwarting our development and relationship success.

As we clear away the static caused by our old wiring, reflection helps to shift and expand our point of view, enabling us to see ourselves, our partners, and our relationship dynamics more objectively. By finding the courage to be present with ourselves, accepting and reclaiming the feelings, needs, and desires that we had been avoiding, we gain access to a wellspring of information.

Reflection helps us further appreciate and understand our core emotional experience and more clearly hear the wisdom that comes from being in touch with our true self. We can then consider a more informed course of action, one that aligns with our intentions and values and helps us get to a better place in our relationships.

Reflecting on our experience also furthers our emotional healing. As we reintegrate previously disowned aspects of ourselves, new feelings can arise in the process. For instance, we may grieve for the self that wasn't allowed to be, for all the time we've been held back from realizing our full potential. We may feel angry on our own behalf that our early conditioning kept us from having the kind of relationships we might have had. In addition, we may feel compassion for ourselves; we may feel a sense of accomplishment or pride for having done something that we'd previously avoided; and we may feel energized or excited about evolving and being able to do things differently.

As psychologist Diana Fosha explains, all of these feelings are signs that we're healing, that we're transforming, that we're moving through our emotional experience toward health and wholeness.[31] We're honoring the truth of our experience, and in the doing, more fully integrating our newfound emotional capacities. We're liberating ourselves from the constraints of our early programming.[32] Our sense of self deepens, and the story of our life expands and becomes more coherent.

On a neurobiological level, when we reflect on our emotional experience, when we think about it and attempt to make sense of it, we engage in a process that links together different parts of our brain and enables emotionally rich knowledge to be organized, consolidated, and integrated into our memory system. In the process, our once rigid and restrictive, internal working models get revised and become more flexible. New information gets imported into our neural networks, and the negative feelings, beliefs, and perceptions of our early learning begin to lose their emotional charge. The reins loosen up to permit a wider range of emotional and behavioral options, thus freeing us up to be able to bring our full and best self to our relationships. Our attachment programming shifts in the direction of earned security and supports us in our development.

But downloading these important updates takes intention, time, and attention. If we don't make a point of stopping to really take in our experience, we won't reap all the benefits our hard work has earned us. As psychologist Rick Hanson points out, by reflecting on what we've learned—holding our felt sense of it in our awareness and focusing on it—we give the power of neuroplasticity a chance to do its thing.[33] We assure that the updates our experiences have generated get downloaded into our neural programming. In short, we use our mind to change our brain.

I'd say that's worth taking a moment or two to reflect, don't you think? After all, what good is an update if it doesn't get downloaded?

Thoughtfully considering the key lessons of our experience while remaining emotionally connected to ourselves both deepens our understanding and maximizes our learning. It gives rise to insight that is not cerebral but one that is firmly rooted in and borne out of our felt experience; the kind of bottom-up insight that can provide a sturdy platform upon which we can take the next step in our relationships toward something better. That's a horse of a different color. That's what we want.

Reflecting on our experience is not unique to Step Three. We make use of reflective skills all throughout the four-step process. When we step back and observe our experience, we are reflecting. We're engaging our prefrontal cortex to help us take a look at and make sense of our experience. Moreover, the participatory-observational stance that is essential to our whole four-step process makes active use of different brain regions as we shift back and forth between experiencing and observing. In this step, we're going to lean a bit more heavily on the reflection side of things. Simply put, having had an experience, you're now going to reflect on it.

When we're working the four steps in real time in our relationships, the amount of time we take to reflect on our experience and figure out how best to respond to our partners may be brief. For instance, we note that we've been triggered, recognize what's at play for us, and respond from a mindful place. At other times, we may need longer. We might need some space to go inside of ourselves and attend to our inner wounds before we can engage with our partners from a more centered, adult place.

The truth is, reflecting on what we learn about ourselves is not a finite process. Rather, it's one that can keep unfolding over time. After all, we're not just reflecting on an isolated moment in time, we're reflecting on how we've been put together, how we've been affected by our early experiences in life, and everything that came up for us in the process.

It's a bit like going on a trip to a foreign country. We leave the safety of our usual routine and familiar surroundings and venture into a new and different world. It's a bit unsettling at first, but it's also stimulating and exciting. While we're there, we have experiences that leave a lasting impression on us that linger in our mind long after we return home. We recall moments from our trip and the feelings they engendered come back to us. We think about what we discovered while we were there and what we discovered about ourselves. Over time, we realize more and more how our experiences changed us and changed the way we see the world.

That's how it goes in this step. That's precisely what we want.

So what can you do to get your reflective juices flowing? Staying close to your emotional experience, you put your mindfulness cap on, so to speak, and consider what you've discovered about yourself and what you've learned. You can ask yourself questions to help make sense of your experience and deepen your understanding. Then you put together the pieces into a narrative that helps to tell your story.

The View from Here

You've been on a journey of self-discovery. By recognizing that you've been triggered and going inside yourself to attend to what is coming up emotionally, you've made contact with a deeper part of yourself, one that you might have not realized was close at hand. Now as you survey the landscape of your experience, everything seems different. Foreground and background have shifted. Things may feel a little wonky and you may feel a little wobbly. That's to be expected. In a way, the dust hasn't fully settled yet. But mindful self-reflection can help you find your footing, and the Triangle of Experience can serve as a guide as you put the pieces together.

In general, the primary players in your emotional experience are the three corners of the Triangle: your defenses, anxieties, and core emotional experiences. By working the steps so far, the light of mindful awareness has helped to illuminate all three of them. What do you see now that you didn't see before? What was going on inside of you that you weren't aware of? How do you understand what happened for you? These are some of the reflective questions you can ask yourself to help you make sense of your experience.

○ ○ ○

They're the same questions I asked Paula, whom you met at the beginning of the chapter. Paula told me about the experience she had with her husband and what she later discovered about herself by leaning into her distress and being open to what her fear had to tell her. Together we did the work of disentangling her feelings, first attending to the scared child inside of her, and then giving her anger, which was at the root of her distress, some room to be felt, moved through, and reclaimed. We then stopped to reflect on Paula's process and what she'd learned through the work she was doing. As we looked back on the interaction she had with her husband and what happened for her emotionally, I asked Paula a reflective question, "What do you see now, that you didn't see before?

Paula sat quietly for a moment, thinking, and then said, "Well I see now that I got triggered when Ivan and I were talking. It made me angry when he was going on about himself and wasn't hearing me. But I'm seeing now just how much my anger kind of freaks me out and how hard it is for me to accept it. I mean, I get worried that something bad might happen if I push for what I want. I feel guilty, like I'm asking for too much, and then I start to question myself. Even though I know on some level I'm not being unreasonable, in the moment I get anxious and drop it. Or at least I try to. But my anger doesn't really go away. I still feel frustrated about the whole thing. I still want something different for us. I just end up feeling resentful."

In this simple response, Paula captures so much. She just described her Triangle-based relationship with her feelings. When her anger starts to emerge along with her desire to assert herself (the "feelings" corner of the Triangle), it's scary to her and she gets anxious (the "anxiety" corner). In response to her distress, she tries to make the feelings go away. She feels conflicted, questions herself, rationalizes Ivan's behavior, and then tries to let it go (the "defense" corner).

Figure 1   **PAULA'S EMOTIONAL DYNAMICS**

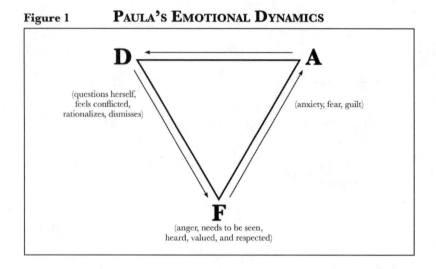

That's the whole Triangle in a nutshell. Paula's just had an up close and personal experience with it. But by observing her emotional process instead of being at one with it, she's able to see what's been going on for her. What was once unconscious is now in her awareness. She gets it now. Her anger and her associated needs to be seen, heard, valued, and respected feel threatening to her based on old internal working models, and they cause a defensive chain reaction that tamps down her emotional response and leaves her feeling fraught and unsettled. Essential aspects of her core emotional experience and herself get omitted.

But why? What's so scary about asserting herself with her husband? Why is it so hard for her to honor her needs and stay the course? Given the work that Paula's been doing to be mindful of her inner experience, the answers to those questions are becoming apparent. Paula can see that her fearful response toward her anger doesn't just come out of nowhere. She now gets that her early experience in life has something to do with it. But we need to make this piece explicit. We need to make sure that her nervous system really understands that the threat no longer exists. We want the past to recede a bit so that Paula can get some distance from it, hear her core self, and feel more firmly rooted in the present. So we crank the reflective camera lens back to enable us to take in a wider perspective. One that includes the details and implications of Paula's past.

"How do you understand your response?" I asked her. "Specifically, why do you think your anger feels scary to you? Why do you feel conflicted about expressing yourself and asserting your needs with Ivan?"

This is what Paula answered:

"Well, I always knew that my mother was hard to deal with when I was younger, but I guess I didn't realize how much my experience with her affected me. She was like a ball of anxiety when I was a kid, always nervous and worried. Anything could set her off. She'd go from zero to sixty in a heartbeat, fly off the handle for no reason, and could be kind of mean at times. We'd get in these giant arguments about something so trivial. I just couldn't understand why she was so mad, why she was yelling. I'd try to calm her down, but there was no getting through to her. No having a conversation.

"Eventually she'd just leave in a huff, go to her room and slam the door or something. She'd ignore me for a while and then act like nothing happened. No apology. No, 'I'm sorry I lost it.' No taking responsibility on her part. It made me so angry. I just wanted my feelings validated. But I'd end up feeling bad and guilty like it was my fault, and, the next thing you know, I'd be apologizing and trying to console her. It was so frustrating and confusing and basically had me walking on eggshells pretty much all of the time she was around. I just did whatever I could do to not to set her off. I just tried to be perfect and stay on her good side.

"I can see now how that made me feel insecure and afraid to trust my own feelings and ask for what I really want. It's so hard for me to let others know when I'm upset. It's like it's in my DNA to not say what's wrong with me, to force myself to smile and be okay, to act like I'm fine. I still struggle with that. Even though I'm an adult, I can still feel like a child, afraid of speaking up, anxious that I've done something wrong, that I've upset someone, afraid that people are mad at me or don't like me.

"It's especially like that with Ivan. Telling him that I'm upset is really hard. The other night was a perfect example. I felt anxious just at the thought of talking with him about how I was feeling, and then when I did and he reacted badly. I got triggered. I felt angry and wanted to assert myself, but I was scared. It's like there's a little girl inside of me afraid of what's going to happen if I do. Like the sky is going to fall, and I'll be all alone. And somehow, I end up feeling guilty and apologizing, like I'm a bad person or have done something wrong. Even though I haven't. It's just like what would happen with my mother. No wonder I cave."

Wow! Paula is really understanding how her early experience in life has affected her. The buzz in her nervous system traces back in time to when, as a child, she had to contend with her mother's anxiety and reactivity. How was she to make sense of her mother's outbursts? What did she think or feel when her mother withdrew? Paula's child mind assumed, as children naturally do, that her mother's behavior had something to do with her. She equated her mother's negative reactions with the threat of rejection and abandonment. To maintain some connection with her mother, she learned to suppress her true feelings, especially her anger.

In these dynamics with her mother, we see the origins of an anxious attachment style. Her mother's unpredictability set Paula on edge, vigilantly monitoring her emotional cues so as to circumvent any potential discord. Consequently, Paula became overly sensitive to the feelings of others and less attuned to her own. Furthermore, her early experience created an internal working model in which anger, assertiveness, and independence were deemed threats to connection, and therefore had to be squelched. Accordingly, Paula unconsciously believed that anger on her own behalf was destructive and shouldn't be expressed, that her needs were not as important as the needs of others, and that should she show her true feelings, she would risk being rejected and abandoned.

Fast-forward thirty years: Paula's brain is still operating by the same unwritten rules; her internal working models are running the show and affecting her feelings, behaviors, and perceptions. Although she takes a risk and asks Ivan for what she needs, she's acutely sensitive to his response. When he starts to get defensive, she understandably feels angry. But her old wiring kicks in, warns her of impending danger, and as programmed, she backs off. Instead of following the lead of her core emotions, she doubts herself, worries that something bad will happen, and feels guilty for causing problems. She feels but she doesn't deal—just what she learned to do to be with her mother.

If Paula had been able to hear Ivan's response without taking it personally and stay rooted in her adult self, or if she had been able to recognize where her anxiety was coming from, calm herself, hear and honor her needs, and then ask for what she wanted, they might have gotten somewhere else. But the past was unknowingly coloring her perception and depriving her of a healthier choice. She was seeing things through the eyes of her younger self, and as such, feeling threatened, powerless, and ashamed.

However, Paula is doing her emotional work; her perspective is shifting and changing. By reflecting on her emotional experience, Paula connects the dots between her past and her present. While it's not news to her that her mother was anxious and challenging to deal with as she was growing up, she's seeing, in real time, the effect it has had on her. She's seeing how her early conditioning has stayed with her, and the subtle and not so subtle ways it shows up: How she's triggered and made anxious by her anger, by her needs to be seen and valued, and by her desire to assert herself, and how she then reacts. How the unwritten rules of her internal working models prevent essential aspects of her emotional experience from being owned, fully felt, and directly expressed.

As Paula so beautifully demonstrates, spending time reflecting on and making sense of our experience takes such little effort, but has powerful effects. Let's take a moment for you to do the same.

REFLECTION EXERCISE

Find a quiet place to reflect on your experience thus far in your process. Think about an emotionally charged interaction you had with your partner, family member, or friend in which you tried to work the first two steps—recognizing getting triggered; noticing your defenses, and trying to put them aside; mindfully attending to your distress; going inside yourself and working through your emotional experience.

Recall how it went for you, what you observed, and what you discovered about yourself. Staying mindful of your emotional experience, consider these questions:

• What do you see now that you didn't see before? What have you learned about yourself? What have you learned about your emotional dynamics?

• How do you understand why you got triggered? What do you recognize as a point of vulnerability for you that can set your early programming in motion?

• What aspects of you and your experience did not feel okay to feel, show, or share? In general, what emotions, needs, or desires feel threatening to your relationship?

• How did your past show up in your present? What early lessons, rules, and beliefs were affecting your current experience?

• In general, what aspects of your emotional experience have felt difficult for you to honor and reveal? How may you have not been honest with yourself and/or with your partner?

What was that like for you? Were you surprised by what you discovered?

Perhaps you found the questions easy to answer. Maybe some of them felt challenging. If an answer to any of the questions didn't readily come to you, that's okay. Being able to reflect on intense emotional experiences is a skill that can take some time to develop. Just allow the questions to linger in your mind and remain open. Bits and pieces will emerge over time, and the picture will flesh out and become clearer. Sometimes unexpectedly we have what psychologist Diana Fosha calls a "click of recognition" where some understanding about ourselves becomes apparent in a deeply felt way.[34] We can see it. We can feel it. We know it to be true.

But mostly it will happen in fits and starts, so keep returning to these questions. Use them as a guide and allow for any others that naturally arise in your process. The main purpose is to make explicit what you've discovered about yourself and allow your awareness and learning to sink in.

As you were reflecting on your experience, did any feelings come up for you? Maybe you felt frustrated or sad as you saw more clearly how your true self had been held back or compromised. Maybe you felt badly for reacting as you had with your partner. Perhaps you felt vulnerable, a bit exposed, or unsure of what comes next. Maybe you felt relieved or hopeful that you're growing in your understanding of yourself. Maybe you felt proud that you're doing the work to turn things around.

These feelings are all part of your healing process. They're a sign that you're deeply engaged. That you're honoring your truth and taking it in. That you care about yourself and your partner. Let the feelings come. Feel your way through them. Allow your experience to be rich. Rest assured, the work that you're engaging in is taking you to a better, more integrated place.

○   ○   ○

Rewriting Our Stories

Let's return to Paula so that you can get an idea of what this process can yield. The more Paula reflected on her experience, the more things made sense to her not just with Ivan, but as far back as she could remember. She saw, with clearer eyes, how her relationship with her mother affected her and shaped the ways she behaved and related with others throughout her life.

In particular, Paula realized why it had always been difficult for her to be assertive in her relationships and advocate for her own needs—healthy capacities that flow from being in touch with and able to make constructive use of anger. Despite being well-liked and having no trouble making friends, deep inside she worried that the other shoe would drop, that sooner or later someone would get mad at her and write her off.

Although Paula hadn't thought she had a problem being angry—after all, she wasn't immune to arguing or complaining with Ivan when she felt frustrated or upset—she was coming to see just how anxious it made her and how difficult it had been for her to trust and be direct about it. As she looked at her relationship history, she saw a repeated pattern, starting with her mother and then proceeding throughout her adult life, in which it had always been hard for her to hear, honor, and express her true feelings with her romantic partners. Worried about the possibility of things falling apart, she often second-guessed herself, let her needs take a back seat, and struggled with being able to say no or set limits. While she might complain, argue, or sulk in her efforts to express herself, ultimately it didn't get her anywhere beneficial.

Overall, her relationships were characterized by a chronic sense of insecurity, frustration, and unsettledness. How could it be otherwise when all along aspects of her true self had been absent from the proceedings? Reflection was shedding new light on her history and a different, more nuanced life narrative was emerging for Paula.

As you reflected on your own experience in the previous exercise, you may have noticed that a story began to emerge for you as well: the story of your past, your present, and maybe even your future. That's understandable. In fact, as psychologist Diana Fosha explains, the emergence of our stories is a natural outgrowth of the kind of emotional work that you've been doing, all the healing that's happening as you open up to, work through, and reflect on your feelings.[5]

As human beings, we have a strong need to make sense of our experiences, our selves, and our lives. It's how our minds work. We want to understand why something happens, how one event relates to another, why people do the things they do, and why we are the way we are. So from an early age, we create stories to help explain, structure, and bring order to our lives. Stories that link the past, present, and future together in a way that makes sense and provides meaning.

When we put our stories into words in a way that goes beyond logic and draws on all of our senses, a coherent narrative of our lives emerges. We make sense of our early experiences and how they've affected us as thinking and feeling come together to weave a life story that is well integrated and rich in meaning, understanding, and emotional depth.

Turns out, that's a good thing. As research has shown, a coherent life narrative is both a marker of a secure attachment style as well as a strong predictor of one's capacity to have healthy relationships. What these important findings suggest is that an attuned and responsive start in life with our caregivers helps us develop the capacity to move through *and* make sense of our emotional experiences. Simply put, our brains can do what we need them to do. The different, specialized regions of our brains are well linked, allowing various forms of information to be processed within and between them and stored in a fully integrated way, one that both reflects and promotes our well-being. That's a good thing.

But for those of us who didn't have an emotionally attuned and responsive start in life, that is those of us with an insecure attachment style, our capacity to process our life experiences adaptively is impaired. The different systems of our brains lack the kind of connectivity that would allow energy and information to flow within and between them and get organized, represented, and stored in an integrated way.

In addition, rigid internal working models constrict our emotional range and exclude aspects of ourselves from our awareness. Implicit memories, and all the unprocessed material they contain, remain locked in time, unavailable for our minds to sort through, resolve, and put in their rightful places on the "over and done with" shelf of our past.

It's impossible to make sense of our lives *truly* with portions of our story hidden in the shadows of our unconscious. The narrative that emerges is like a novel that has sections missing. It doesn't hang together. It doesn't make sense. In addition, our story can't get beyond the surface facts when we're cut off from our feelings. It reads like an outline, void of any substance. Nor can we string together the plot points of our lives in a logical sequence when the emotional charge of unprocessed memories disrupts our thought process and throws us off balance. We can't formulate a coherent life narrative, nor can we be a fully integrated and emotionally whole person.

But you're doing your part to turn that all around. The work of the last two steps enabled you to uncover hidden layers of your story, and thus of yourself. By observing, staying with, and working through your internal experience, your core feelings, needs, and desires are becoming apparent and available to you. Implicit memories that heretofore have been covertly coloring and shaping your present moment experience are becoming conscious. Essential pieces of your story are getting uncovered and made explicit. Now with mindful reflection you can integrate them with what you already know and weave it all together into a coherent life narrative. In the doing, you not only help to shift the way you see and understand yourself, you also improve the way your brain functions.

That's right. When done well, telling our stories changes our brains. By attuning to our felt experience, as we've been doing in our work so far, we help to even out the neural pathways between our lower and higher brains and foster *vertical* integration. Top-down and bottom-up lines of connection and communication are brought into balance. Making sense of our lives facilitates right-left, side-to-side, or *horizontal* integration. It grows and strengthens connections between the two hemispheres of our brain by bringing together the narrator function of our left brain with the autobiographical memory storage of our right brain.

The process of mindfully reflecting on, and making sense of, our lives can help us achieve the same kind of integrated brain wiring a secure attachment experience early on in life would have afforded us. We can update our internal working models to allow for more adaptive ways of being and can move our insecure attachment style toward earned security. We can free ourselves from the prisons of our past and bring our best selves to our relationships. We can become the authors of our own lives.

In the end our life experiences, regardless of how challenging or traumatic they may have been, are not as important as whether we've made coherent sense of how we've been affected by them. That's where freedom lies.

So what do you need to do? Similar to what you saw Paula do earlier in this section, you need to step back from your present moment experience, put the pieces together, and tell the story that brought you to this place in your life. Reflect on what your early attachment experiences were like and how they affected your development. Trace the themes that run through the events of your life and find the connections that link them together. Note the repeated relational patterns that have followed you all the way into adulthood. Take the time to make sense of your experience and put it into words.

It's not easy to tell this tale. It takes courage. As you look back in time, you'll start to see the ways in which your needs were not met, the ways in which you may have been neglected or mistreated, and feelings can arise in the process, feelings that you have for yourself and perhaps toward your caregivers.

But by staying open and allowing yourself to honor and move through your emotional experience, you further your healing. You integrate the truth of your life, and a new story unfolds and settles into place; one in which you can see yourself more objectively and with compassion; one that allows the past to recede and enables you to land more fully in the present; one that reflects and supports your becoming emotionally integrated and whole.

Writing can be a useful tool in helping construct a coherent life narrative. If you simply reflect on your experience without trying to put it into words, you're liable to skip over details or avoid particular areas without even knowing it. But when you try putting pen to paper, or fingers to keyboard, the blocks or gaps in your story are more likely to become apparent. You'll notice when the words stop, when they don't flow. You'll notice when you become agitated and want to get up and leave. You'll notice when you have a hard time finding your way.

These are helpful cues. They're alerting you to something inside that needs to be attended to in order for it to be understood and articulated, in order for the block to be worked through, or the gap to be filled in. They're keying you in to unprocessed issues, feelings, or memories lying under the surface. They're pointing you in the direction of work that needs to be done. In this way, writing can help you see what you might not otherwise notice.

When we write, we hold ourselves in a more mindful way. We stay present to ourselves, waiting patiently in the empty space until we find our next word. We listen and care about what we say. If the words don't feel right, if they don't ring true or capture the essence of what we're trying to communicate, we work to find the words that do. We become more intimate with ourselves as we endeavor to connect with what's inside us and reveal our truth.

As psychiatrist Mark Epstein points out, this way of being with ourselves is similar to how an attuned parent is with her child.[6] She tunes in and listens, she supports and cares. Her presence is calming and regulating. She provides a safe environment in which the child's true self can emerge. When we write, we nurture a secure attachment with ourselves. Perhaps then it should come as no surprise that research by psychologist James Pennebaker has shown that expressive writing calms physiological reactivity, improves our sense of well-being, and positively affects how we connect with others.[7]

That's all good stuff which you can now put to use in this next exercise. If writing is just not your thing, try talking into a voice recorder and transcribing it afterward. That's likely to have many of the same benefits.

LIFE NARRATIVE EXERCISE

Make some time to reflect on your life story. Find a quiet place, free from distractions, where you can be present to yourself. Start by thinking about your current relationship experience. Staying close to your feelings, consider what you've been learning about yourself and your relationship struggles. Sit with that a moment. Take a deep breath and let it out. Notice how it feels inside of you.

Then when you're ready, whether in writing, typing, or speaking out loud, tell your story. Tell it to yourself. Tell it as though you're conveying it to a trusted other. Someone who you really want to know what your experience was like.

Look back in time and describe what your experience growing up in your family was like. Describe what your parents were like. What your relationships with them were like. Explain why you think they behaved the way they did. Describe what you had to do to adapt and make those relationships work. Take your time and allow room for your feelings. Allow the words to arise from a deep place. Feel your way through and pause when you need to.

Moving forward in time, trace over the events of your life noting how your early conditioning in your family showed up in your other relationships. Note how it affected the ways in which you think and feel about yourself. How it shaped your beliefs. How you see and experience others. How you've behaved. Note the patterns or themes that run throughout your relationship history up until the present.

Give yourself lots of room to find your way. Let one thought or feeling lead to another. Notice what memories come into your awareness. Welcome them. Take time to be with them and whatever feelings they may bring. Pieces of your story are falling into place. Stay open and allow the path forward to reveal itself.

Be gentle with yourself as you allow the words to come from a deep place inside you. When feelings arise, give them plenty of room. Stay with and move through them as you've been learning to do. Use the breath to regulate your experience so that you can remain comfortably within your window of tolerance. Allow the story to unfold. Allow your feelings to unfold. Allow the words and feelings to come together naturally.

If the next place to go in your story doesn't readily reveal itself, give it time. Don't stress about it. You

can always circle back and fill in the blanks
as more information arises.

If the going gets hard, if it feels like too much,
take a break. You don't need to muscle your way
through it. After all, it's a long story and needs
time to be told. It's also a living, breathing story;
one that will continue to expand and deepen
throughout your life. As you have new experiences,
new realizations and insights will emerge that can
be folded into the rich tapestry you are weaving. Do
the work that you can do now, and then time and
time again return to your story. Continue to tell it.

Through your process, try to hold yourself with
care and compassion. Tell yourself that what
you're doing is important. You're honoring your
experience. You're furthering your healing. You're
becoming a more fully integrated person. Knowing
yourself in this deeper way will enable you to find
the courage to be open to knowing your partner.

Honoring Your Truth

Taking the time to reflect on your experience is likely bringing you
some clarity. You're taking in what you've been learning. You're
deepening your understanding of yourself. You're growing in your
awareness.

With this clearer vision comes choices. Do you continue to
stay on the path you've been following? Do you continue to let your
life experience be determined by your early conditioning? Do you
continue to deny essential aspects of yourself? Or do you take a risk
and try something different? Do you shake off the trappings of the

past and allow your authentic self to show up? Do you give your relationships the chance for something greater?

Chances are, you want the latter. Otherwise you wouldn't be here. You wouldn't have come this far. But understandably, the next step in your process can feel challenging. It requires you to cross a bridge into a strange new land, one in which you allow yourself to be vulnerable and more authentic with your partner. You'll share parts of yourself that heretofore have felt off limits. You may feel unsure and not quite certain of which way to turn, but if you listen to your feelings, they're showing you the way.

When we are mindful of our emotions, we discover their inherent wisdom. When we pay attention to them, we find the help we need to move forward in our lives. In simple and clear messages, our core feelings provide us with essential information. They signal to us when something of importance, something that matters to us, is at stake. They tell us what we need, what we want, and what we would prefer. And they organize and motivate us to follow a course of action that will get us to a better place. As Daniel Goleman writes in his seminal book, *Emotional Intelligence*, "All emotions are, in essence, impulses to act, the instant plans for handling life that evolution has instilled in us."[8] Our core feelings ready us to respond, and like a compass, point us in the direction we need to take.

By listening to our feelings, we sense what we need and how we should respond. For instance, when we feel afraid in our relationships, it's telling us that our connection with our partner is feeling threatened in some way; we need reassurance and to regain a sense of security. It prompts us to reach out to our partners and find our way back to safe connection. Sadness or hurt tells us that we're experiencing a loss of some kind, perhaps we're not feeling valued by our partner. It's telling us that we want to be seen and appreciated, that we need to be treated with respect, and it's prompting us to express our hurt to seek comfort and care.

Figure 2   THE WISDOM OF OUR FEELINGS

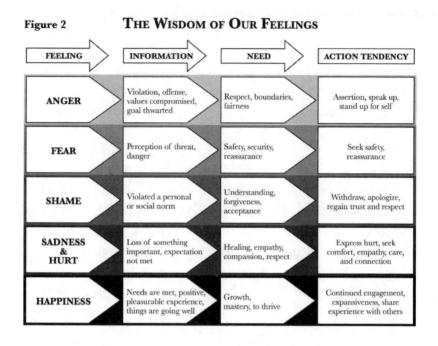

FEELING	INFORMATION	NEED	ACTION TENDENCY
ANGER	Violation, offense, values compromised, goal thwarted	Respect, boundaries, fairness	Assertion, speak up, stand up for self
FEAR	Perception of threat, danger	Safety, security, reassurance	Seek safety, reassurance
SHAME	Violated a personal or social norm	Understanding, forgiveness, acceptance	Withdraw, apologize, regain trust and respect
SADNESS & HURT	Loss of something important, expectation not met	Healing, empathy, compassion, respect	Express hurt, seek comfort, empathy, care, and connection
HAPPINESS	Needs are met, positive, pleasurable experience, things are going well	Growth, mastery, to thrive	Continued engagement, expansiveness, share experience with others

All of our core feelings operate this way (see Figure 2[9]). All of them provide us with helpful guidance and give us an idea of how best to navigate our experiences with our partners, how to make our relationships better, and how to love. As couples therapist Sue Johnson explains, "Learning to love and be loved is, in effect, about learning to tune in to our emotions so that we know what we need from a partner and expressing those desires openly."[10]

○ ○ ○

Throughout Paula's story you may have noticed glimmers of her truth. It showed up when she felt distance in her relationship with her husband and wanted to address it. It was there when she leaned in and tried to talk with him. It was in the anger she felt when her needs weren't being heard, valued, or respected, either by Ivan or by her mother when she was a little girl. And it was there when she felt motivated to make another attempt to express her feelings and needs to her husband and to find a productive way forward. On some level, she heard it, but her old wiring kept her from trusting and honoring it.

When we're in a reactive state our core emotional experience gets distorted, and we can't hear our truth. But by cultivating the capacity to be present with ourselves, we can move through our feelings and find it. We can do the work to calm ourselves, shift into a receptive state, and connect with it.

When we drop inside ourselves and stay with our emotional experience, allowing our core feelings the time and space they need, we can sense our truth. We can also feel it and get what psychologist Eugene Gendlin called a "felt sense."[11] Our body, or the emotional and physical sensations that we experience, key us into it. They let us know whether the choice we're considering feels wrong or right for us; whether the action we're thinking of taking is in line with our best self, the self we want to be. When we get ourselves back to a more emotionally centered place, we can hear it more clearly. Something inside of us clicks into place—we feel a shift, and we see the path before us.

As psychologist Diana Fosha explains, by connecting with our emotional truth, we align with our "essential self, our core self, the self that has been there all along waiting," and we think to ourselves—*this is me.*[12] We're then able to respond from a deeper, wiser place inside of us.

Let's take some time to practice clarifying and connecting with your truth.

WHAT'S MY TRUTH?

Take a moment to ground yourself. Settle in and find your center. Then recall a recent experience with your partner in which you felt triggered. If you're not currently partnered, you might use an experience that you had in a past relationship, or one with a family member or friend. Try to look at it from a distance. What was going on for you? What caused you to get triggered? Recall the experience and watch it unfold. See it all the way through to completion. Let yourself land on the other side of it.

Looking back on that experience, what emotions were coming up for you? Beneath your defenses and distress, what were you feeling?

Perhaps, in hindsight, the feelings may already be clear to you. If not, that's okay. Drop inside yourself and try to sense into them. Hang in the open space and see what materializes. Maybe you were feeling afraid, hurt, angry, or ashamed. These tend to be the feelings that get our old wiring activated. Or maybe you feel something else. Consider the different feelings and see what rings true to you. When you sense the truth of your experience, you'll likely notice a shift of the energy in your body. Take a moment to sit with this awareness. Breathe it in. Let it be deeply felt.

Staying close to your felt experience, ask yourself then: What are my feelings telling me? What are they telling me I need? What do I want? What am I feeling motivated to do? Allow the answers to come from within you, from your feelings, not from your head. Take some time to be with what emerges. Notice how that feels. Sense whether the answers ring true to you.

If anxiety or nervousness starts to creep back into the picture, name it to tame it. Recognize that it comes from an old place. It's an echo of your childhood, an experience that you already have

> lived through and is long over with. Tell yourself
> that your feelings matter and you are free to feel
> them now, unlike when you were a child. They're
> important for you to listen to and take seriously. It's
> okay for you to honor your truth. Nothing terrible
> comes from owning your truth.

What Truly Matters?

Once we sense our truth, we need to make good use of it. We need to lean forward and begin to put our feelings into words. We need to open up with our partners.

If the prospect of relating with your partner from an authentic place makes you feel anxious—and I'm guessing that it does—I understand. I really do. I remember what it was like for me when I started to push myself to be more emotionally honest in my relationships. Just the thought of doing so, of letting my partner, family members, or friends know when I felt afraid, hurt, or angry, made me nervous. It still can at times, though far less so. But—and this might sound odd—that's actually a good sign. Our anxiety is telling us that we're attempting to do something out of the ordinary. That we're approaching something that we typically avoid. That we're about to venture outside of the confines of our internal working models so that we can more fully inhabit the present moment. We're taking a risk and anything that feels risky can make us nervous.

It's also a sign that our relationships matter to us.

Deep inside, all of us want to have loving connections. All of us want to have successful relationships that are mutually satisfying. That's what has motivated us to do all the work that we've been doing thus far in our process. But anxiety and fear can keep us from taking that next step and trying something new with our partners. Getting in touch with our relationship values can help give us the nudge we need to move forward.

What do I mean by values? Simply put, I'm talking about what matters to you. Not what you think should matter, not what others seem to think should matter, but what truly matters to *you*.

Think about it, deep down inside, what do you want for yourself? What do you want for your relationship? What kind of partner do you want to be? These are important questions. But if we're honest with ourselves, chances are we haven't given them much thought. While our relationships are the most important things to us in our lives, how much time have we actually spent thinking about how we want them to be?

In general, we think a lot more about what we *don't* want in a relationship. But that can actually be a good starting point.

O   O   O

Over the years, when I would visit with my parents, who have been married for over fifty years, I would witness for the umpteenth time the tension that could easily flare between them; harsh tone that they could sometimes take with each other, and how defensive they could sometimes be. A classic example of what happens when two people—one with an avoidant attachment style, the other with an anxious attachment style—remain trapped by their early programming and never find a way to earned security. The experience was both disturbing and sobering for me. I saw firsthand how I might have ended up had I not found the help I needed to begin to address and alter my early conditioning. In a painful way, being around them helped to clarify and strengthen a personal value of mine which is to be someone who treats their partner with kindness and respect, and to be someone who is able to express himself in a sensitive and caring way.

While these particular values of mine might seem like standard operating procedure to some, they haven't always been easy for me to uphold. Growing up in a family where bickering between my parents was a frequent occurrence did not exactly wire my brain to support an even, steady, and mindful communication style. Suffice it to say, cultivating such a way of being has been a work in progress for me.

I've had to take an honest look at myself and recognize that some of the styles of interacting that I acquired early on in life needed work. In turn, I've had to develop and continue to practice the skills of emotional mindfulness.

Furthermore, while I'm bothered by how my parents would sometimes behave with each other, and though I don't want that for my relationship, it hasn't been enough for me to simply acknowledge that. I've needed to clarify what I truly want for my relationship consciously and then commit to making it happen.

You see, when we're not explicit about what we want for our relationships, when we don't consciously choose the principles by which we want to live, we don't have a strong enough rudder to help guide us, especially when the waters get rough. Our old programming gets the best of us and our actions get out of sync with what we want for ourselves. When we get clear about what our values are, when we claim them and set an intention to uphold them, they can become a source of guidance and motivation.[13]

For instance, I don't particularly like exercising, but I do it more days than not. Why? Because I value my health. Both physical and emotional. Especially as I'm getting older. I know that exercising improves my physiology, bolsters my brain chemistry, and may add some years to my life. At least, I'm hoping it will. When I start to contemplate not going to the gym, which happens pretty frequently, I get an uneasy feeling inside. I think about my cholesterol levels, I think about my mood, I think about my sleep issues. I think about what matters to me, and before you know it, I'm packing my gym bag. My values motivate me to keep going.

In addition, if we're explicit about our values and then behave in ways that are not in line with them, we know it. We feel it. We get disappointed with ourselves. We feel regretful, guilty, or ashamed. Sure it's not pleasant to feel these feelings, but that's their point. They're letting us know that we're getting off track. When we're able to stay present to them and listen to the messages they convey, they can be helpful to us. They prop us up, get us back on our feet, and keep us moving forward.

With all this in mind, let's take a moment to consider your relationship values and what it might be like to let them guide you.

WHO DO I WANT TO BE?[14]

Take some time to reflect on what is important to you in terms of your relationship. Consult your deepest sense of truth and think about how you would like to be as a partner. If there was nothing holding you back, if you could be your best self, if you were free to wear your heart on your sleeve, what would that look like? What sort of relationship would you have? Ask yourself:

• What's important to me in my relationship?

• What kind of partner do I want to be?

• How do I want to behave in my relationship?

• How do I want to relate with my partner?

• What personal qualities do I want to cultivate?

• What sort of a relationship do I want to have?

Carefully consider each of these questions. Be honest with yourself. There are no right or wrong answers, there is only your truth. Make you answers explicit. Write them down so that you can look at them and reflect on them.

Allow yourself then to imagine what acting in line with your values would look like. Think about the last conflict that you had with your partner in which you were triggered. If your best self had been leading the way, how would it have gone? If you acted in accordance with your values, what would that have looked like? What feelings, needs, or desires might you have communicated? What might you have said or not have said? What might you have done differently?

Perhaps it's difficult for you to imagine. You may not feel as though you have a frame of reference to draw on. But chances are if you think about it, you have had moments where your best self has been in the lead. Look back on your life and think about it. Let your mind open up to remember yourself in all your goodness. Maybe there was a moment with a friend, maybe with a family member, a coworker, or maybe even with your partner. Recall what that was like. Let yourself acknowledge and take in that you have the capacity to live by your ideals.

If it's still hard to imagine, think about someone you know who lives by their values in a way that you admire. Think about what they're like. Think about what qualities they possess that you appreciate. Imagine them behaving in a way you admire and notice how you feel in your body. Let yourself feel what it might be like to be them. What it might be like to have these qualities yourself. Try imagining behaving in a similar way.

By imagining acting in accordance with your values, you're actually shifting your internal working models toward healthy relating. You're developing a frame of reference in your mind that you can draw on when you need it. You're setting yourself up for success.

○　○　○

One Step at a Time

Let's take a look at what happened for Paula. Through reflection, she could see that her anxiety about asserting herself was rooted in her past. While this awareness didn't necessarily free her up immediately, it helped to put things into perspective for her. She understood that the distress that she could feel in her relationship with her husband was part and parcel of having developed an anxious attachment style and not an indication that she was in any kind of danger. Instead of getting distracted by it, which had so often been the case, she began to see how her getting triggered was actually a signal that she was having a core feeling, need, or desire that she needed to pay attention to. An essential aspect of herself that at one time felt forbidden was needing some help to be brought into the light, appreciated, and shared.

It wasn't easy at first, but slowly over time Paula found the courage to honor the truth of her emotional experience and let it guide her. She found the courage to lean in and share more of herself with Ivan. In the doing, her truth became clearer, her sense of self felt stronger, and her connection with Ivan grew more secure. That's what she wanted for herself, and that's what she wanted for her relationship.

You can do the same. And like Paula, you don't have to do it all at once. That's not a requirement, nor is it a reasonable expectation. Stretching into the fullness of your being and sharing it with others is a process. So be gentle with yourself. Start slow and take it one step at a time.

Perhaps at this point in your process, you might just acknowledge to your partner that you're feeling activated and need a moment. Or you might acknowledge that you're feeling vulnerable and are having a hard time expressing yourself. That you want to be present and open but are finding it challenging. Or you might try to begin to put your feelings, needs, and desires into words. To express mindfully what's going on inside of you, what you're feeling, what you need.

Any of these options are good. Any of them are a healthy next step. Any of them will help to move your relationship in a positive direction.

CHAPTER TAKEAWAYS

- Reflection helps us reintegrate core feelings, needs, and desires back into our emotional repertoire.

- Reflection enables emotionally rich knowledge to be organized, consolidated, and integrated into our memory system.

- Thoughtfully considering the key lessons of our experience while remaining emotionally connected to ourselves both deepens our understanding and maximizes our learning.

- A coherent life narrative is both a marker of a secure attachment style as well as a strong predictor of one's capacity to have healthy relationships.

- Mindfully reflecting on and making sense of our lives fosters healthy neural connections in our brain.

- Reflection helps to update our internal working models and move our insecure attachment style toward earned security.

- Our core feelings provide us with essential information that helps us see how best to respond in our relationships.

- Our relationship values can be a source of guidance and motivation.

CHAPTER SIX

Step Four:
Mindfully Relate

*"Love takes off the masks we fear we cannot live without
and know we cannot live within."*

JAMES BALDWIN

"What's the matter?" Blake's wife asked, sounding more frustrated than concerned. "You haven't been listening to a word I've said. I'm trying to talk to you, and you're a million miles away."

Blake felt his body tense up. He wanted to continue staring at the television screen and act as though he didn't hear her. He wanted to break into a case of beer and drink himself into oblivion. He wanted to hop online and escape into fantasies of "no strings attached" encounters with women who'd shower him with praise and expect nothing in return. He wanted to blurt out, "Nothing's the matter! Can't I just relax in peace? But he knew where that would lead. They'd spend the rest of the night arguing and get nowhere for it. Besides, deep down he knew it wasn't true.

Work was stressing him out. Not that anything was going badly. In fact, it couldn't be better. But despite all evidence to the contrary, it often felt to Blake as though he was just a hair's breadth away from it being found out that he wasn't all that he seemed cracked up to be. He was haunted by the distant voices of people who'd once told him that he'd never amount to anything and couldn't shake the feeling that the positive regard he consistently garnered somehow wasn't real or deserved.

He wanted to confide in his wife, share his insecurities and fears with her, open up and not feel so alone, and find reassurance. He wanted to hear that she believed in him and that it would all be okay. But he was afraid of what she might think. Afraid that he'd seem foolish or weak.

Blake wanted to tell her how awful he felt that they were having such a hard time. He yearned to reach out and bridge the chasm between them but felt afraid that she would reject him. Afraid that no matter what he did, or how hard he tried, he'd get it wrong. That he'd never be able to please her or ever be good enough.

He wanted to tell her how much he loved her. How much he missed her and longed to be close. To talk openly. Share his feelings without holding back. Find a way to something better for them. But it all felt so scary. So overwhelming. Allowing himself to be emotionally vulnerable went against everything he learned growing up. All the messages he got as a child to suck it up and be strong, to stop crying or he'd be given something to cry about, to quit complaining and just get on with it.

It was if every fiber in his body had been telling him, "No, don't do it!" Well, not exactly every fiber. Something was pushing its way to the surface and trying to get through. Something was aching to be known and expressed. Like a tiny blade of grass inching its way up through a crack in a concrete sidewalk, new life was poised to emerge.

What should I do? Blake wondered to himself and then turned to his wife and said. . .

○   ○   ○

Opening Up

Blake has come to a fork in the road. A choice point that has significant implications for the future of his relationship. Will he continue to play by the rules of his old programming and stay trapped in a dynamic that only leads to isolation and suffering? Or will he take a small step forward down an unworn path and begin to share more of himself with his wife? Will he stretch beyond the confines of his old internal working models and find a way to engage with her that brings them closer together instead of further apart?

The work of the last three steps in the previous chapters may have brought you to a similar place on your emotional journey. By slowing down the action, working with your feelings, and clarifying your emotional truth, you've afforded yourself a precious opportunity, one that's filled with possibilities. It's in this precise moment that you can change the course of your relationships.

But taking advantage of this opportunity can feel quite challenging. It requires a leap of faith. It requires taking a risk. To go against the dictates of your early conditioning and do something different. To open up and reveal sides of yourself that you long ago learned to hide. To directly express the core feelings, needs, and desires that you've been too afraid to share.

It can feel scary. That's to be expected. We're confronted with the fear of the child within us that somehow learned that expressing aspects of ourselves is dangerous and will threaten the security of our relationships. But it's only in facing our fears and seeing our way through to the other side that we can diminish their existence and dispel their power. That we can learn, once and for all, that our world will not come to an end, that we will not be destroyed. We may need to do some work to get the conversation moving in a constructive direction, but it's only in facing our fears that we can develop new ways of relating. We can then leave the past behind and cultivate a more loving connection with our partner. We can have the kinds of new experiences that will update our old programming and rewire our brain for the better.

When we're emotionally authentic and open, relating with our partners in a manner in which we both feel safe and heard, we sow the seeds of security, which as you know is the basis for a healthy relationship. We lay the groundwork for a solid foundation, one that supports and promotes our growth as a couple. Feeling secure in our connection, we can weather the challenges that inevitably arise in a relationship and feel confident that we'll not only be okay, but that we'll be better for it. Our bond deepens and strengthens over time and our love grows. We change ourselves, and we change our relationships.

As world-renowned meditation teacher and author Sharon Salzberg explains, real love requires that we "open to our wholeness rather than clinging to the slivers of ourselves represented by old stories. Living in a story of a limited self—to any degree—is not love." [35] Relationship security cannot be developed when one or both of us has a wall up, whether it be a wall of silence or a wall of noise. Security grows when we step out from behind the safety of our defenses and allow ourselves to be vulnerable with our partners. When despite our fear or hesitation, we show up "wholeheartedly"[36] in all our vulnerabilities and imperfections and do our best to be fully present and responsive to each other. When we hang in and do our part to see things through and get us to a better place. That's what makes the difference. That's the essence of loving like we mean it.

Speaking of vulnerability, as the saying goes, "it's all relative." In general, revealing an aspect of ourselves that may be perceived as weak or shameful causes us to feel vulnerable. For instance, expressing our hurt, sadness, or fear. Sharing our needs for reassurance, support, and understanding. In addition, expressing our anger, asserting ourselves, setting limits, and having boundaries can make some of us feel vulnerable, especially when such behaviors were met with negativity when we were younger. Similarly, feeling proud of ourselves, expressing joy or wonder can also make some of us feel vulnerable. Whatever the feeling, need, or desire, our fears trace back to our own unique experiences early in life. They're sides of ourselves that we learned were dangerous to express. They're sides of ourselves that feel vulnerable to share with our partners.

To show up in our entirety requires courage and skill. We need to be able to stay present and balanced, to understand and manage our feelings, and to sensitively, honestly, and coherently express ourselves. In addition, we need to be attuned to our partner and responsive to their emotional experience.

Now it just so happens that most of these capacities are ones that we've been growing all along. They are the skills of emotional mindfulness. However, the work we've done so far has been internal—attuning to and working with what's going on emotionally inside of ourselves. In Step Four, "Mindfully Relate," we expand the circle of awareness to include both our partner's emotional experience as well as what is happening between us. In addition, we weave in and cultivate our innate ability to empathize with our partner's emotional experience—to feel and understand what they're feeling. The better we get at empathizing with our partner's feelings, the better we'll be at recognizing and getting beyond their defenses and avoiding getting caught in old, unproductive patterns of relating. In short, the better we'll be at moving our relationship in a positive direction.

Bringing together the practices of mindfulness and empathy has powerful benefits for ourselves and for our relationships. As psychotherapist and mindfulness teacher Linda Graham explains in her book *Bouncing Back*, this dynamic duo effectively grows our capacity for resilience.[37] By helping to strengthen the functioning of our prefrontal cortex, we're better able to observe our experience and see our way out of embedded patterns of relating, respond more flexibly and adaptively to relationship challenges, and open up to a broader range of options. In addition, the synergy of mindfulness and empathy gives rise to an inner wisdom that, when we listen to it, can guide our choices and actions toward exploring healthier ways of relating. Just what the doctor ordered!

While the next step in this process may feel daunting, you've been working up to it. You're well prepared. You've already done so much work to make what lies before you with your partner a more constructive experience. You have a better grasp of what's been going on for you emotionally and have strengthened your capacity to be present with and listen to yourself. You just need to be able to express yourself and navigate your interactions with your partner in a more mindful way. That's doable.

Of course, your partner plays a role in how things will go between you. If they're not ready or able to be receptive, if their defenses continue to get the best of them, it will likely be challenging for you. But while you can't control how they'll respond or whether they'll take responsibility for their behavior, you're not without influence. You can do your best to express yourself in a manner that will maximize your partner's ability to hear and receive you, you can stop yourself from responding in a manner that fosters tension and discord, and you can support them in ways that help get you back on track as a couple.

Too often, we underestimate our partners' capacity to be receptive, and we shy away from communicating our feelings altogether. We don't even try and thus deny ourselves the possibility of something better. While it may not always go as smoothly as we'd like, we can learn in the doing. We can improve our ability to stay present, attuned, and empathic with them. And we can grow from our experiences and efforts. We just need to be willing to open up and give ourselves a chance to find out what's possible.

Who knows? You just may be surprised. Let's find out.

Mindful Speech

Something happens. Your partner makes a comment or behaves in a particular way, you see an expression on their face, you hear something in their voice—and bam! You get activated. Your old programming kicks in. But this time instead of business as usual, instead of shutting down or spinning out of control, you catch yourself. You recognize that you've been triggered, calm your distress, and attend to what's emotionally going on inside of you. You connect with the core feelings, needs, and desires that have been trying to make themselves known.

Meanwhile, your partner is looking at you, eagerly awaiting a response. They want to know what you're feeling, what you're thinking, and although it may not seem like it in the moment, they want to connect.

You need to find a way to let them in on your emotional experience; try to express directly what has heretofore been left out. You need to bridge the gap between the two of you and put your feelings, needs, and desires into words. Your choice of words is crucial, as is the manner in which you express yourself. And yet perfection is not needed. You just need to do it in a way that fosters a healthy exchange, one that will be constructive and inspires connection rather than conflict.

Seem like a tall order? It certainly can feel that way when you're getting started. Especially when you're attempting to share aspects of yourself that make you feel particularly vulnerable. But like any other new behavior, the more you do it, the easier it becomes. And you don't have to do it all at once. You can take it slow. You can talk about your feelings a little bit at a time. In fact, doing so can make the experience more manageable both for you *and* for your partner. The process of developing and deepening emotional intimacy is a bit like peeling an onion—we remove and expose one layer at a time.

As you begin to share your feelings with your partner, it can help to start by saying a few words that ease the tension of the moment, move communication forward, and help your partner feel more receptive. John Gottman, a renowned expert on relationship dynamics, suggests that a "soft-start up" to a difficult conversation— one in which we proceed in a gentle and compassionate manner— can have a positive impact on how it will end up going.[38] In particular, conversations that start off gently are more likely to end that way, as opposed to those that start off harshly. A harsh start often tends to bring more of the same.

With this sage advice in mind, you could begin to talk with your partner by acknowledging a simple truth—that it feels scary to talk openly and reveal more of yourself to your partner. For instance, you could start off by saying something like, "This is hard for me . . ."

or "I'm feeling nervous about sharing my feelings . . . " or "I'm not sure how best to talk about this . . ." Or you could express your desire to have a conversation that is constructive for the both of you. You could say, "I'd really like to try to talk with you about this in a way that will be helpful to us." You could also explicitly accept responsibility for playing a role in your relationship dynamic, stating that you're not blaming your partner or implying they're at fault. You could say, "I know I'm responsible for a part of what's going on here. I accept that and want to understand how I can do things differently." Any of these options would make for a softer startup.

Drawing on our work in the last three steps, you can talk then about your emotional experience. You can begin to share the feelings, needs, and desires that heretofore have been difficult for you to express.

Now here's another instance in which the Triangle can serve as a useful guide. You can use it to help put your emotional experience into words—to explain what's happening for you and why. Starting at the top of the Triangle, you can acknowledge that you were triggered—that you felt anxious or uncomfortable and perhaps got defensive—and explain why. Then you can share what feelings were coming up for you.

For instance, if Blake, whom you met at the beginning of this chapter, were to open up in this way to his wife, he might say, "When I hear you sounding frustrated, I get anxious and tense up. It's like a part of me wants to run, to escape, and I end up zoning out. I actually want to talk with you. I want to connect. But I'm afraid of how you'll react. I'm afraid of what you might think of me. I guess, deep down inside I feel ashamed, like there's something wrong with me and I'll never be able to get it right. That you're going to be disappointed no matter what."

In his response, Blake started at the top of the Triangle by sharing elements of his emotional experience that are closer to the surface (feeling uncomfortable, tensing up, zoning out). He then made his way down to the bottom of the Triangle to reveal the feelings and desires that were hidden behind his defensive reaction (fear of being rejected, feeling ashamed, desire to connect). In this way, Blake was explaining his reaction to his wife, helping her understand what was going on for him emotionally. He allowed her to see a more vulnerable side of him, one that wasn't readily apparent.

PUTTING YOUR EXPERIENCE INTO WORDS

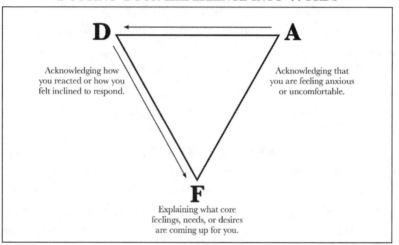

D

Acknowledging how you reacted or how you felt inclined to respond.

A

Acknowledging that you are feeling anxious or uncomfortable.

F

Explaining what core feelings, needs, or desires are coming up for you.

Notice that Blake used the language of "parts" to describe his desire to flee when he said, "part of me wants to run." Talking in this way can be very useful. It can make it easier for us to acknowledge aspects of our emotional experience that we may feel bad about. In addition, it helps to use the layered quality of our emotional experience to explain to our partners that there's more going on with us than meets the eye. For example, we may look angry to our partners, and that may be all they see or feel, but in reality our anger is only one aspect of our emotional experience. Underneath, there's a range of feelings. We may also feel hurt, lonely, scared, hopeless, helpless, embarrassed, ashamed, inadequate, rejected, and so on. When we use the language of parts, we convey the multifaceted nature of our emotional experience. We help our partners see us in more depth.

Similarly, we could talk about our inner child and explain how part of our reaction comes from a young place inside of us. For instance, when talking about his fear with his wife, Blake might say, "it's like there's a scared kid inside of me who's worried about how his parents are going to respond." In addition to giving us a way to communicate and explain our emotional experience, such a disclosure can shift our partners' perspective and reaction to us. Instead of seeing only our frustrated, tense, or distracted adult-self before them, they get a glimpse of our younger self, they see the child inside of us, and suddenly something shifts for them. Their defenses melt. They get it. They understand what it's like to feel vulnerable and small. Where only a moment ago resentment and frustration crowded the scene, a ray of empathy shines through and they feel for us. They feel different toward us.

Furthermore, when we talk about our child-self, we are communicating our awareness that our present moment experience is in part being colored by our early conditioning. We're helping our partners understand the roots of some of our relationship struggles.

To that end, as the conversation with your partner progresses, you might talk with them about your early life experience. You can share with them a bit about what things were like for you growing up and the lessons you learned through interactions with your caregivers. You don't necessarily have to go into depth all at once. After all, this is the type of "getting to know you" conversation that evolves over time in relationships. You might start off simply by saying something like, "It wasn't okay in my family to be _____ (sad, afraid, vulnerable, angry, have needs for affection, reassurance, attention, and so on)." Or, "Whenever I expressed my feelings/needs, my father/mother would _____." Or, "I remember one time when _____." You could then go on to explain how the same fears you experienced as a child show up for you now, and while you understand rationally that your fear is old, nevertheless you can still feel vulnerable and respond defensively. In the doing, your partner gets to know you better, develops a better understanding of your struggles, and may be inclined to share about themselves as well. You both benefit.

At some point, you will need to find a way to let your partner know what you need from them. This part can feel particularly challenging. After all, it's one thing to express your feelings, it's another to ask for something from your partner and make your needs known. Doing so can make you feel even more vulnerable. It's a risk. You're not sure how they'll respond. And once again, you come up against the dictates of your old programming—the early learning that told you it's safer to keep your needs to yourself.

But think of it this way: how is your partner supposed to know what you need from them unless you tell them? They're not mind readers (despite our wishing they were!). They're probably as confused over the matter as you may be. They want to be helpful, they want things to be different between you, but they're not sure what to do to make that happen. And they may also be coming up against the limits of their own attachment wiring and have their own fears that are getting in the way. When you tell them what you need, you're helping them; you're making it easier for them to know how best to respond. So try to be clear and simply state what you need, such as, "I really want/need/could use your_____" (reassurance, understanding, comforting, care, respect, acceptance, to feel valued, loved, and desired, and the like).

Overall, as you talk about your feelings, needs, and desires with your partner, your aim should be to communicate in a way that both minimizes the chances that they'll get defensive and increases the likelihood that they'll be able to hear and receive what you're trying to express. Using "I" statements (e.g., "I am feeling hurt," versus, "You're upsetting me"), talking about how you *feel* rather than what you *think* ("I feel hopeless" versus "I feel like you're never satisfied, no matter what I do") and describing what is happening rather than blaming or judging ("When I see you checking your phone while I'm talking with you . . . " versus "You're so insensitive!") can make what we're trying to say easier to receive. In addition, asking for what you need rather than telling your partner what to do or making a demand will likely yield a better response. A good rule of thumb is to imagine how you'd feel hearing whatever you're trying to express if the shoe were on the other foot.

While mindfully choosing your words is important, the tone in which your words are conveyed can be even more crucial. Are you relating with your partner from a place of care and concern, or are you approaching them with an edge? Talking about difficult matters goes so much better when it's done in a spirit of kindness and care. In fact, research shows that when negative feedback is delivered in a warm, supportive tone, the receiver invariably leaves with a positive impression of the exchange.[39] This doesn't mean that we don't address unpleasant feelings. But we do it in a way that's constructive and "supports the growth of your relationship" As Julie Gottman, co-founder of the Gottman Institute, explains, "You can throw spears at your partner. Or you can explain why you're hurt and angry, and that's the kinder path." [40]

Often when we are willing to share the feelings behind our defenses, the energy of our conversation shifts, a space opens up between us, and we enter a different way of relating with each other. What felt impossible when our defenses were leading the way now feels possible. We see what we need to do to shift our experience. We see what we need to do to get our relationship back on track. And the more we allow ourselves to open up and be vulnerable with our partners, the stronger we become at relating in this way.

○ ○ ○

Seeing with a Beginner's Mind

When Blake's wife complains to him about his seeming to be "a million miles away," what is she trying to say? Beneath her apparent frustration, what is she feeling? What is she wanting from him? All that Blake hears is the critical tone she takes. His body tenses up and he scrambles to find an escape route. He goes into flight mode.

But how would it be if instead Blake were to notice his impulse, pause, and take a moment to consider what might be going on for his wife below the surface? What if he looked past her defenses and wondered about what she might be feeling more deeply. Maybe he'd realize that behind the angry mask she wears lies a longing to connect and a fear of losing him. What would that be like for Blake? How would that affect his feelings toward her? How then might he respond?

Just like us, our partners were shaped by their experiences with their caregivers and continue to be unknowingly affected by their early programming. Just like us, they're afraid to be vulnerable, to express their true feelings and let us see them in their entirety. Just like us, they're afraid that we'll be critical and dismissive. Just like us, they're afraid that they won't be enough. Just like us, they're afraid that they'll be rejected and abandoned. Somehow we don't realize that about them, or we do but we momentarily forget. Such is the case when we're in a reactive state. All we see are our partner's defenses, the ways in which they learned to contend with their fears—their coming at us with frustration or their retreating behind a wall of silence. We zero in on what we perceive to be a threat and lose sight of everything else.

To make matters worse, our perceptions of our partners aren't always accurate. We often view them through the biased filters of our internal working models. Our early conditioning causes us to be hypersensitive to certain emotions and less aware of others. We see certain things in an exaggerated fashion and miss others.

For instance, studies show that those of us with an anxious attachment style have amygdalae that are more easily activated by negative feedback, such as a look of anger on our partner's face. In contrast those of us with avoidant attachment style are less responsive to positive feedback, such as a smile.[41] In a way, especially when we are upset or triggered, we see what our implicit memory is looking for. At those times, our assumptions and expectations seemingly confirmed, we end up viewing our partners in a limited way and fail to see the totality of their being. And at those times, we most certainly don't see whatever made us fall in love with them in the first place.

Of course our partners play a role in our relationship dynamics. It's not like they're blank slates upon which we project all our fears and anxieties. The manner in which they engage with us matters and can be provocative. But what if we could remove the filters of our implicit programming so that we could see our partners more clearly? What if we could shake off our preconceptions, look past their defenses, and begin to see them anew? Well, we can. The practice of mindfulness affords us this possibility.

When we are mindful and can get some distance from our reactivity, we can bring to our experience what Zen master Shunyru Suzuki called "beginner's mind" and see it with fresh eyes. No longer constrained by previous held beliefs, we can come to our experience with openness and curiosity and discover other points of view. As Suzuki explained, "In the beginner's mind there are many possibilities, but in the expert's mind there are few."[42] Don't our partners and our relationships deserve that opportunity? Wouldn't that be a loving thing for us to do?

To that end, let's take some time to practice looking at our partners and at our experiences with them with a beginner's mind.

REFLECTION

Think about a recent experience with your partner that was emotionally charged. Choose one that is representative of the kind of relationship conflicts you typically experience with each other. If you're not currently partnered, think about a past relationship, or a relationship with a close friend or family member. Try to step back and look at the experience as an objective observer. Encourage yourself to let go of any preconceptions or prior beliefs and give yourself the opportunity to get to know your partner in a different way. If at any point, you find yourself getting emotionally activated or start to feel defensive, take a moment to calm yourself and come back to center.

As you think about the experience, recall how your partner responded. Did they complain and get critical, or did they pull away? Did they turn up the volume, or did they go silent? It might help to look over the list of relational defenses in Chapter Three and see which seem familiar to you. Which describe your partner's behavior in this instance? Which do you typically encounter with them?

Next, in your mind's eye, try putting your partner's defenses to the side, so that you can consider what might have been going on for them under the surface. In other words, let yourself get curious about what core feelings, needs, or desires might have been coming up for them that they were too afraid to share with you at the time. For instance, might your partner have been feeling hurt, afraid, ashamed, or angry? Might he or she have wanted comfort, reassurance, or validation? Let your mind open up and consider any and all possibilities. Are they feelings that your partner typically shares with you, or sides of him or her that you rarely see?

Next, let yourself wonder why it might be hard for your partner to show you these feelings. Is there some way in which you tend to behave that makes it more challenging for them to open up? Or have they always been that way? Remember how you experienced them when you first met. Now consider what you know about their early history. What were their relationships like with their caregivers? How might their experiences growing up help

explain their reticence to be more emotionally
open with you? How might their early
conditioning be showing up in your current
interactions? (If you don't know much about your
partner's early life, consider having a conversation
with them at some point, one that will likely
evolve over time. When this kind of exploration
is done in the spirit of curiosity, understanding,
and compassion it can be a healing experience for
both of you and bring you closer.)

Take some time to reflect on all the different
possibilities that occur to you. Do any of them
ring true? Do any of them seem possible? Notice
how each of them makes you feel. Notice how
they make you feel toward your partner. Allow
the new information and the feelings it engenders
to have an impact on you. "Sit with" your
emotional experience and try to really take it in.
Allow it to be deeply felt.

What was that like for you? Did other ways of seeing and understanding your partner emerge? Did anything new or different occur to you? Might there be sides to your partner that have been difficult for you to see, appreciate, and acknowledge? How do the possibilities affect your perception of them? How does it make you feel toward them?

Perhaps you hadn't quite realized that your partner is also struggling emotionally. That he or she may also be afraid of being present with you in a more authentic way. That the manner in which she or he typically responds may actually belie a deeper truth. Maybe you hadn't thought about what else might be going on for your partner, what other feelings might also be at play. We tend not to think about these things in the heat of the moment. But we should.

Because when we do, we increase our chances of getting what we long for in our relationships.

Allowing ourselves to get a broader perspective on our partners helps us see them in a fuller way. We see our similarities, not just our differences. We get a glimpse of the person inside of them that's been held captive by fear. We see how we're both wanting to get to a better place. We see how we're both longing for love and connection.

We need to bring this awareness to our interactions. We can pause and reflect and remind ourselves of what our hearts—and calmer minds—know to be true. Then we can try to meet their defenses with curiosity, openness, and compassion. Doing so would benefit us both.

Listening with Our Hearts

What if Blake were to try to put his wife's comments to the side for a moment and listen to her with his heart? What if he were to drop inside of himself and get a felt sense of *her* emotional experience? Perhaps he'd discover something altogether different? Maybe he'd hear her despair? Maybe he'd sense the sadness and fear she feels when he seems to disappear? Maybe he'd notice her longing to connect? How would he then feel toward his wife? How might that affect how he reacts to her? Chances are he'd respond to her in a softer way, avoid getting into an argument, and by doing so make it easier for their interaction to move in a positive direction. That would be a positive start.

If Blake were to listen to his wife in this way, he would have tapped into his innate ability to empathize—to sense, feel, and understand what others are feeling. Empathy is what enables us to see, know, and love another, as well as feel seen, known, and loved by another. Not surprisingly empathy is a key component in successful relationships. And mutual empathy is what makes all the difference. Everybody wins!

We're all capable of empathizing with others. We're all born with the capacity to do so. Remember, we come into the world highly attuned to our caregivers' emotions. We can tell what they're feeling, and they can do the same. That's empathy in action. It's how we communicate with each other. It's how we connect. As psychiatrist Daniel Siegel explains, "It's how we come to 'feel felt' by one another."[43] But if we're not mindful of our emotional experience, if we're cut off from our feelings or overcome by them, if we're in a reactive state, we can't make use of this essential skill.

Feeling empathy for others starts with being able to be emotionally present with ourselves. When we're open to our own feelings, when we're attuned to them, we can more easily *resonate* with someone else's emotional state. That is, we can mindfully sense in our own bodies what another person is feeling. Our ability to be able to feel what another is feeling may be due in part to what have been referred to as "mirror neurons," a type of brain cell that may enable us to understand the actions, intentions, and emotions of another person.[44] As their name implies, mirror neurons apparently get activated both when we experience an emotion ourselves as well as when we witness someone else experiencing an emotion. So when we see our partners feeling sad, angry, happy, or afraid, for example, our mirror neurons light up, and we feel similarly. We *resonate* with their emotional experience, and we mirror them, or feel what they are feeling.

That's a good start. It viscerally tunes us into another person's feelings. But empathizing with someone requires more than merely resonating with their emotional state. We need to examine their experience and consider their point of view. We also need to get the thinking part of our brain, the prefrontal cortex, involved and make sense of their feelings. We need to put ourselves in our partner's shoes and try to understand how it feels to be them. If we don't, we may resonate with their feelings but not really understand where they're coming from. Or we may respond on an emotional level without thinking and confuse their feelings with our own. Thus, when we get our whole brain engaged, both our limbic system and our prefrontal cortex, "mindful empathy"[45] is both a physiological as well as a mental process.

Therefore, while the capacity to empathize is innate, in order for us to make good use of it, we need to be emotionally mindful. We need to be attuned to and present with our emotional experience. *And* we need to pay attention to our partners so that we can sense and understand their feelings as well. We need to listen to them, not only to their words, but perhaps more importantly, to what they're communicating nonverbally—through their facial expressions, their tone of voice, and their body language. We need to give them a chance to express themselves and hear them with our whole being.

Of course, it's harder to do these things when we're triggered. When that happens, it's difficult to make good use of our feelings or to see our partners clearly. We can't quite tell which feelings are our own and which belong to our partners. For instance "Is this my fear or his?" "Is this her anger or mine?" How often, when we get past the heat of the moment, do we look back on our exchanges with our partners and feel differently toward them? Do we feel a sense of empathy for them that had somehow eluded us only moments before? When we calm our reactivity and drop inside ourselves, we can connect with those feelings in real time. When we slow things down, and stretch the space between stimulus and response, we can see things more clearly. We can find our truth, and we can sense into our partners' truth as well. In doing so, we tap into our capacity to empathize.

Making eye contact with our partners can enhance our ability to empathize as the eyes and the muscles around them convey one's emotions. We read someone's emotional state in part by looking at their eyes.[46] When we look at our partners' eyes, the brain regions that enable us to more accurately process their feelings and intentions get activated. Even brief moments of eye contact can clue us into our partners' feelings and help us get emotionally "in sync."

But making eye contact can also feel intimidating. Not only is making eye contact an extremely intimate thing to do, it can also activate our implicitly stored memories and our fears about emotional connection. We anticipate that our partners will react similarly to the ways in which we were responded to in our past. We expect that we'll be rejected, dismissed, or shamed. We're afraid of what we'll see in their eyes, so we avoid looking at them.

But when you avoid eye contact, understandable as it is, you miss an opportunity to confront and possibly disprove your old fears. You miss an opportunity to see the truth of your experience. Instead of disdain, you may see a longing to connect. Instead of anger, you may see hurt and vulnerability. And instead of fear, you may see tenderness. What would that be like? How would that change your emotional experience? When you find the courage to look, the fullness of your partner's being can come into focus, and if all goes well, your past fears can begin to fade. Your old programming can get a necessary update. You can see your partners more objectively and empathize with them.

When we tap into our empathy for our partners, it benefits both of us. Our view of them expands. We see beyond their defenses to their inner truth. We recognize and identify with their vulnerability and fears. Our defenses soften, our fears subside, and our heart opens. We hear the wisdom of our core self and intuitively we know what to do to make things better. Compassion flows, and we feel inspired to respond to them in a more loving way. We're both the better for it.

To that end, below is an exercise to help you enhance your ability to empathize with your partner.

LISTENING WITH YOUR HEART EXERCISE

As you interact with your partner, try
practicing the following:

Try giving your partner your full attention.
Let him or her express themselves without
interrupting them. Put judgment aside and let
yourself get curious. Listen to what they are
saying but also to the feelings beneath the words.
As he or she is talking, tune into your body and

try to sense what your partner is feeling. Let your mirror neurons do their thing.

Pay attention to your partner's nonverbal cues (e.g., facial expressions, tone of voice, body language). Notice what happens inside you when you do. Notice what you feel in your body. Let yourself make eye contact with your partner, even for brief moments. Notice what you see in his or her eyes. Notice what happens for you emotionally when you do.

With a felt sense of your partner's emotional experience, consider why they're feeling the way they're feeling. Try to imagine what it would be like to be them. Put yourself aside and consider their perspective. Notice how you then feel toward your partner as you do. How are you inclined to respond? What is your inner sense of what would be the best thing to do for both of you?

If you're having a hard time connecting with your partner's emotional experience, try picturing him or her as their younger self. See that child's face in your mind's eye. Look into her or his eyes and notice what happens inside of you. Notice what happens in your body. How do you feel toward that child? How does that make you feel toward your partner? How do you feel inclined to respond?

Then, if you're so inclined, share your understanding of your partner's emotional experience with him or her. You might say, "I'm getting the sense that you're feeling_____." And then ask for feedback, "Did I get that right?" See if it rings true for her or him. If it does, notice

> how your partner responds emotionally to being
> seen in this way, having his or her experience
> reflected back to them. Notice how that makes
> you feel. If your understanding of their feelings
> wasn't quite accurate, allow yourself to take in the
> feedback with curiosity and not with resentment
> at being corrected or devastated for being wrong;
> if your sense of them does not quite resonate in
> this moment, ask your partner for clarification
> and ask them to help you better understand their
> experience. Your partner will likely appreciate your
> interest and care, and your wish to really know and
> understand her or him.

What was that like for you? How was it for you to try to empathize with your partner's experience? To put the thinking part of your brain aside for a moment and listen with your heart? To allow your felt sense to inform your understanding of your partner? To allow it to inform your understanding of your relationship dynamics? Has your point of view changed? If so, how? Imagine what it would be like to carry this heartfelt knowledge of your partner with you and to draw on it the next time you experience a conflict in your relationship. How might things go differently?

○   ○   ○

Mindful Interactions

Let's come back to Blake.

Should Blake find the courage to open up to his wife, he has a number of options.

He could just share with her how he's feeling in the moment— stressed, overwhelmed, wanting to escape.

He could let his wife know how he hears the words she's saying and isn't sure what to make of them.

He might apologize for being distracted and empathize with her feeling upset about the distance between them.

He might let her know how he wants to connect with her as well but that he isn't sure how.

He might acknowledge that deep inside he feels afraid.

And, then what? What should Blake do next? Well, it depends on how his wife responds. Does she soften and open up, or does she continue to complain? Is she able to hear him, or do her defenses get in the way? It could go either way. The two of them have been getting caught in a particular dynamic for so long that it may be hard to shift gears. It may take a few tries before they're able to change course and move in a different direction.

So what is Blake to do? How should he handle whatever comes next? How can he maximize the possibility that their exchange will move in a positive direction?

In order for things to go well when we interact with our partner, we need to be mindful of a number of different things. First, there's our own emotional experience. We need to be attuned to and manage our emotional experience and do our best to try to stay in an open, receptive state. We also need to be attuned to our partner, listen to what they are saying, sense and understand what they feel, and respond wisely. Moreover, we need to keep an eye on what's happening between us. Are the lines of communication open or have they shut down? Are we working together, or are we now at odds? Is energy flowing, or has it come to a stop?

If we're not mindful of these different streams of awareness—what's happening inside of us, what's happening with our partner, and what's happening between us—we can get derailed. It's no wonder that our interactions with our partners can be so challenging!

Practicing emotional mindfulness is key. We do that by making sure our observer is online so that we can mindfully navigate all the different pieces that come into play when we interact.

Once again, the Triangle can offer us invaluable assistance in this regard. In addition to helping us track our and our partners' experience, we can use it to understand how things are going between us and figure out what to do. For instance, at any given moment, we can recognize whether the channels of communication between us are open, closed, or somewhere in-between, and in the doing, get a good idea of how best to proceed. In this way, the Triangle becomes a communication "traffic light" of sorts, helping us to know when it's best to *stop, wait, or go*.

Drawing on the work of mindful communication expert Susan Gillis Chapman, we can view each corner of the Triangle as representing a different color of a traffic light (see Figure One).[47] For instance when one or both of us become reactive while we're engaging (the defense corner of the Triangle), we can imagine that the light has turned red. That's telling us that communication has shut down, on one or both sides of the conversation, and it's time to stop and regroup. In contrast, when both of us are emotionally open and in a receptive state (the feelings corner of the Triangle), we can imagine that the light has turned green, and it's safe for us to continue opening up and sharing. And when either of us is on the verge of getting triggered (the anxiety corner of the Triangle), we can imagine that the light has turned yellow. That's a sign that we need to slow down and proceed with caution.

The traffic light imagery helps us identify the different states of our communication experience and to be aware of the consequences of each. At any moment in time, while we're interacting with our partners, we can look to the Triangle for guidance about how best to proceed.

MINDFUL COMMUNICATION TRIANGLE

Defenses   Anxiety

Feelings, Needs,
Desires

When the Light Turns Red

At some point, as we try to talk and share our feelings with our partners, we may get too activated to be able to proceed in a constructive manner. Our threat alarm goes off, and our defenses kick in. We may pull inward or close off. Or we may push back, argue, or say something hurtful. When that happens, it's a sign that the light has turned red. We are in self-defense mode, no longer seeing clearly and no longer listening to our partners or ourselves. The lines of healthy communication have shut down. In moments such as these, the best thing we can do is *stop*. We need to take a break and calm our internal activation. We need to get ourselves back to a more centered state before we're going to be able to move forward in a productive manner.

Just how much time we may need to stop and collect ourselves depends on what's going on for us emotionally. Sometimes we just need a brief moment to calm our internal activation and get centered. We can pause, ground ourselves, take a deep breath, and let it out slowly—whatever we need to do to calm our distress—

and then gradually make our way back into the conversation. But sometimes we may need a bit longer. We may need to take more time to attend thoroughly to whatever has gotten emotionally stirred up for us. When that's the case, we can draw on our "Stop, Drop, and Stay" tools to work through our feelings and take care of our inner child. When we're clearer, when we've separated out what's past from what's present and are feeling more balanced, we can return to the conversation.

Whether we pause briefly or take an extended time out, it's best to let our partners know what's happening for us and that we need to stop. Generally, it's not a good idea to "exit" a discussion with our partners prematurely and without offering an explanation. Doing so would likely provoke them and only make matters worse, especially if they're also feeling activated. We can avoid creating any unnecessary distress by letting our partners know where we're at. We can tell them we just need a moment. We can explain that we're feeling triggered or overwhelmed and need to take a break. We should also assure them that we're not dropping the conversation, that we intend to come back to it when we're feeling more centered and can reengage in a constructive manner, one that's better for our relationship. And of course we need to do just that.

The Other Side of Red

The red light also comes on when our partners get activated—when their defenses take over, and it's clear that they're not about to budge. That's a sign that they're in threat mode, no longer able to listen to us or take us in, and that healthy communication is not going to be possible. That's a clear sign that we need to stop. But it's one that we often miss. Why? Because when our partners get defensive, our alarm bells go off as well, and in a flash, our lower brain threatens to take over. We get activated. Our partners say something critical and we feel the urge to retaliate or argue our case. Or they withdraw and we get upset and go running after them. Before you know it, we're up to our old tricks.

But if we can bring mindfulness to bear on the moment, we can prevent that horse from leaving the gate. We can recognize what's happening for our partners and for ourselves and rein in our defensive response. We can pause to calm ourselves and consult with the voice of wisdom inside of us. Intuitively, we know that no good will come from getting caught up in a defensive dance. No one wins. When we're mindful, we can make use of this precious knowledge in real time. When we're mindful, we know that the best thing we can do, on behalf of ourselves, our partners, and our relationships, is to suggest that we stop.

Just how we make this suggestion is important as well. Given our partner's activated state, we'd do best to use the language of "we" rather than "you." As in, "We should probably take a break" versus, "You need to take a break." See the difference? Even though we may not have become reactive, using the language of "we" instead of "you" is gentler and likely to go over a lot better with our partners. They're less likely to hear it as an accusation or that they're being blamed in any way. Rather, it communicates that we're holding the relationship in mind, that we're in this together, and that we're not opponents. That's a more loving approach.

When the Light is Green

The light turns green when we're in a receptive state. Our defenses have eased up and we're able to be emotionally vulnerable. The lines of communication are open, and energy is flowing in both directions. We're able to listen to ourselves and to our partners. We're able to be emotionally present and connected. Our hearts and minds are engaged and working together. In short we're feeling and dealing while relating.

This is the state that emotional mindfulness and the work of the four steps helps to grow. By staying mindful, by maintaining a balance between observing and participating in our experience, and by continually bringing ourselves back to the present moment, we're able to engage in a receptive way.

The green light tells us that it's safe to continue moving forward. Our task is to seize the opportunity. To take risks and share more of ourselves. To explore new ways of being and connecting with our partners. And to use our mindfulness skills to steady our ship and stay the course.

But as we anticipate moving forward into unchartered emotional territory, we may not realize we've gotten a green light. We start to feel anxious or afraid and react as though we're in danger. But usually, that's a sign that our old programming is showing up a bit. Our nervous system hasn't yet adjusted to doing things differently. We haven't had enough constructive experiences with our partners to know that we're in a safe zone. The only way we can really find out that conditions are fine is for us to lean forward and give opening up a try. We need to push through our initial anxiety so that we can come more solidly into the present moment and see that we're okay, that it's going to be fine. The more we do that, the clearer it will be when the light is green. In fact we'll likely discover that the light is more often green than we had realized.

The reality is that being in the green light zone is not without moments of discomfort, tension, and anxiety. It's inevitable that we'll feel that way when we take a risk to be vulnerable with our partners. Or when they take a risk to be vulnerable with us. When we express difficult feelings or try to address challenging issues. But when we engage with our partners in a mindful way, when we attune to both our and their emotional experience, and do the work to stay regulated, the light stays green. And that's just what we need to do. We need to continue to use our mindfulness tools to abide with any discomfort that arises and move through it. To attune to our partner's experience, to stay present and open to them, and to be sensitively responsive. In the doing, we stretch our emotional tolerance and expand the green light zone.

The Other Side of Green

Speaking of stretching, what happens when our partners risk being vulnerable and open with us? Do we open up further in response? Do we welcome their emotional expression with open arms? Does our light continue to stay green?

One might think that it would be a watershed moment when the very thing we've been wanting from our partners comes to fruition—their defenses soften and they show a different side of themselves. It can be. Our partners open up and share their longing, their hurt, their sorrow, or their love, and we feel it. It moves us.

But sometimes staying present to our partner's feelings can be challenging. Sometimes, in addition to the good feelings that arise for us in response, we encounter painful emotions as well; unprocessed feelings from our past that have been buried inside us. For instance, as we take in our partner's tenderness and care, up comes the sadness and pain of times when our needs weren't met, when we weren't seen, valued, and loved in the way we longed for. The exact opposite of what's happening in the moment.

Although the contrast of feelings can cause a mini internal crisis of sorts, it's actually a good thing. In his book *The Mindful Path to Self-Compassion*, psychologist Christopher Germer refers to this process as "backdraft," which is what happens when a firefighter opens a door to where a fire has been burning, and as the oxygen rushes in from the outside, there's a burst of flame.[48] Similarly, when our hearts open up to take in emotional nourishment, when we receive our partner's love, tenderness, care, or validation, painful feelings can sometimes be released. The painful feelings are leaving us as we make room for the new.

Our work in these moments is to stay present, receive, and abide with the feelings that come. To feel the sense of being seen, understood, cared for, and loved, while allowing for the sadness and pain over not having had those things in the past. We do the work of staying, breathing into the tension and constriction so that it opens up, and riding out the painful feelings as they leave us. We develop what psychologist Diana Fosha refers to as our "receptive affective capacity": our ability to receive the emotional offerings of our partners—their care, empathy, encouragement, recognition, and love.[49] In the doing, we change our relational programming; we update our internal perception of our partners, ourselves, and what we can expect in our relationships.

We owe it to ourselves to take in the good and to let ourselves heal the pain from the past. And we owe it to our partners. They need to feel their impact on us. They need to feel received. We all do. We all need to feel felt. We all need to feel and know that we exist in our loved one's heart.

When we're in the green light zone, we're able to give as well as receive. Although it may feel challenging at times, there is a sense of rightness and truth, that what's happening between us and our partners is constructive. That we're getting somewhere better.

We need to be mindful of that. We need to recognize that something positive is happening, and we need to acknowledge it. We need to tell them that we appreciate being able to talk in this way. How we're able to be vulnerable and open with each other. We need to let them know how much it means to us when they let us in or give us room to be heard. That we're grateful for their understanding, their sensitivity, and their care. Recognition and affirmation fosters more of the same and widens the green light zone.

When the Light Turns Yellow

The yellow light comes on when we're on the verge of being triggered. Something pushes our buttons, and our nervous system springs into action. If we're not paying attention, if we're not tuned in to what's happening for us emotionally, we miss it. We don't see the light turn yellow. We don't notice that we're starting to feel uncomfortable, that our heart rate is speeding up, that our breathing is getting shallow. We don't recognize the signs that would tell us that we're getting activated. We zoom right past them and end up in the red light zone—in a *fight-flight-or-freeze* response. And, well, you know how the rest of that story goes.

All the work we've been doing so far has been about stretching the space between the yellow and red lights—the space between stimulus and response. When we can do that, we can recognize that we've gotten activated and calm ourselves down, find our footing, and get back into the green light zone. We can continue to engage with our partners and avoid going down a dead-end street. That's what we need to do when the light turns yellow.

As you know, the key to recognizing what's emotionally happening for us is in paying attention to our felt experience, what's happening in our bodies. When we're mindful of our internal state and sensitive to the signs, we can tell when we're getting activated. We can tell when energy is rising inside of us. In those moments, we need to call on our anxiety regulating skills. For example, we can recognize and label what's happening for us, we can pay attention to our breathing and slow it down, and we can ground ourselves by observing our experience.

Here's another way we can give ourselves a literal helping hand when the light turns yellow. It's a simple yet powerful technique; all we need to do is locate the place in our body where we're feeling activated and put one of our hands on it.[50] We might put a hand on our chest, our stomach, our side—wherever we're feeling a sense of tension, constriction, or agitation. Doing so is calming and grounding. It's like we're letting the activated part of us know that we're paying attention. That we see it and hear it. And that we're going to be okay. We're letting it know it can settle down. That we're not in danger. That we're able to handle the situation. It's as though we're separating out our adult-self from our distressed inner child, so that our core self can lead the way.

Once we've taken the edge off a bit, we can then talk about what's happening for us. We can describe what we're experiencing instead of being at one with it. We can acknowledge our impulses to lash out or shut down without acting them out. Doing so calms our nervous system and helps us to feel more balanced and in control. We get our observer engaged and assure that the right and left hemispheres of our brain are working together.

So instead of letting your distress get the best of you, observe it and put it into words. You can say something like, "I notice that I'm getting activated. Something's coming up for me, but I'm trying to stay calm." Or, "I'm starting to feel defensive, and I don't want to get ahead of myself or misspeak." You could use the language of parts and say, "Part of me wants to run, but I'm trying to stay present." "I think the kid inside of me is getting a little worked up. He's afraid that _____." And you could give your partner feedback about their impact on you by saying, "I want to be able to hear what you're saying, but the way in which you're talking to me right now is making it challenging for me," "When you don't respond, I get anxious. I start to feel afraid that I'm losing you in some way," or "I get triggered when you don't seem to be valuing what I am saying."

As you're talking, you can slow down your pace and lower the volume. Both help to regulate our internal experience. When we're getting activated, it's typical to talk more quickly and to get louder. Both are signs that our nervous system is revving up. Speaking slowly and more softly can help to move it in the other direction. In addition, it deepens our connection to ourselves, and helps us to feel more centered.

The Other Side of Yellow

Of course the yellow light can also come on for our partners. Something happens between us, and they start to get activated. We can sense it, we can see it, we can feel it. While they're ultimately responsible for attending to their own inner experience and regulating themselves, we can help them out. Especially when it's obvious that they're having a hard time. Doing so benefits both of us by helping to keep our experience anchored in the present moment.

So you can say something. You can acknowledge what's happening for your partner and suggest slowing down. You can say, "It seems as though you may be having a reaction. Let's just slow down and take our time." You can express the empathy you feel, "I sense that you're feeling afraid right now (or anxious, hurt, vulnerable, and the like), and I feel for you. I want to help. I want to support you." You can simply suggest that you both pause and take a moment. Working pauses into our conversations can give us both space to be reflective and come back to center. You can also give them some time if they need it before proceeding. In addition, you can talk to them in a calm, soft voice, and slow down your rate of speech since doing so can be calming for *their* nervous system as well.

We can also try to be mindful of the ways in which we impact our partners, the ways in which our reactions and behaviors affect them. For instance, if we get activated and seem to be shutting down or on the verge of lashing out, our partner's attachment system may spring into action. Based on their own programming, he or she may read what's happening for us as a threat and can get triggered.

When we're mindful of these dynamics, we can ease our partner's distress by telling them what's happening for us. For instance, if you get quiet, you can reassure them that you're not withdrawing, but that you need a moment to think. Or you can explain to them that although you may have sounded angry, you're actually feeling vulnerable or anxious inside. Being sensitive in this way to your partner's experience can go a long way toward helping them stay in the green light zone. And you both benefit.

Paying attention to the emotional dynamics that occur when we interact with our partners affords us greater control over how they'll go. When we're attuned to what's happening between us, we can make better choices in terms of how we respond. We can stop when the light turns red. We can slow down and proceed with caution when the light turns yellow. And we can freely move forward when the light is green.

Being attuned to these dynamics is a skill that we can grow. The more we do it, the better we'll be at discerning where we're at as we communicate with our partners, and we can steer the experience in a helpful direction. So seize the opportunity to practice tracking your experience whenever it arises. Throughout your day as you interact with others, even in low stress situations, pay attention to how you're feeling. Notice what the energy is like. Notice whether the channel of communication feels open, closed, or somewhere in-between. Notice whether you're getting a green, yellow, or red light signal. On whose side of the interaction is it? Yours? The other person's? Or both? Repeatedly observing these dynamics without judging them will help cultivate mindfulness in your interactions with others that you can draw on when relating with your partner.

Leaning In

Sharing more of ourselves with our partners can be challenging. It feels uncomfortable. But it is precisely this discomfort that tells us we're on the right path. It's showing us where we're stuck, where we've been holding back. It's showing us where fear has been getting in our way and thwarting our potential. It's showing us where opportunity lies. We need to recognize its message and lean into it. We need to find a way to move through the discomfort and show up in our relationships in our entirety. To express the core feelings, needs, and desires that we've been too afraid to share. That's the path toward health.

We don't have to do it all at once. We can lean into our discomfort and share our feelings a little at a time. When the discomfort eases up a bit, and it will, we can lean in a little further and share a bit more. We can use our mindfulness skills to ease the way. We can slow ourselves down. We can notice what's happening in our bodies, what's happening for our partners, and what's happening between us. We can keep grounding ourselves in the here and now and then lean in a little further. Over time our capacity to be present emotionally with our partners will expand and our fears will subside.

Opening up with our partners, letting them see us in our entirety, is an act of love. As Brené Brown points out, "We cultivate love when we allow our most vulnerable and powerful selves to be deeply seen and known."[51] We honor ourselves and our loved ones. We create the kinds of relationships with our partners we were meant to have. We become the people we were meant to be. We leave the past behind and come more fully into the present.

O O O

Such was the case for my client Blake who you met earlier in the chapter. He seized the moment. He stuck his toe in the water and embarked on an emotional journey, one that would transform him and his relationship with his wife. What did he do? He emotionally opened up. He leaned in and began sharing his feelings with his wife. The emotions his old programming had told him were off limits. His worries, his fears, his disappointment, and his sadness.

It's not that it wasn't challenging at times for Blake. It was. Sometimes he and his wife would fall back into their old patterns of behavior. Sometimes their defenses would get the best of them. But inevitably, after the dust settled, Blake would come back around and continue onward, and to his wife's credit, so did she. They both kept leaning in, sharing more of themselves, letting the other in. Over time the tension they had frequently felt between them subsided and was replaced by a deep sense of connection, closeness, and security.

Now, looking back in time, Blake is struck by the changes in him. No longer constrained by his early conditioning, he experiences himself, his wife, and his relationship very differently. He explained, "I feel like my wife and I are partners now, on an equal footing, whereas in the past I felt as though I was a child and she was an authority figure. I was afraid to let her see what was inside of me or express how I felt. I just wouldn't do it. But now it's totally different. I don't feel judged. I don't have to hide. Now it feels safe. Now I can say, 'I'm feeling this or I'm not feeling that, or this is what I need.' I would have never done that before."

Then as Blake reflected on how he once felt compelled to try to escape his feelings, he drew on his knowledge of mechanics to describe his experience. He said, "I guess I thought I could run really fast through my feelings and not be affected by them. But that's a bit like trying to slice through liquid. You can't. You can swipe your hand through it, and for the first second you can part it, but it always closes back in on you. That's how it was with my feelings. They always came back around. The pressure really never went away.

"Now, I don't need to run through them. I don't need to escape. I can be still and feel them move through me. Now I can just be. I can just be me. And it's fine."

CHAPTER TAKEAWAYS

- A "soft startup" to a difficult conversation can have a positive impact on how it will end up going.

- When expressing our feelings to our partners, we can use the Triangle of Experience to help put our emotional experience into words.

- Using the language of parts or referring to our inner child can make it easier for us to talk about our feelings with our partners and helps to convey the complexity of our emotional experience.

- As we share our feelings with our partners, we should aim to communicate in a way that minimizes defensiveness and maximizes receptivity.

- Coming to our experience with a "beginner's mind" can help us to see our partners with fresh eyes and discover other points of view.

- Empathy is what enables us to feel, see, know, and love one another and is a key component in successful relationships.

- Making eye contact enhances our ability to empathize as the eyes and the muscles around them convey one's emotions.

- When we're interacting with our partners we need to be mindful of our own emotional experience and our partner's emotional experience, as well as what's happening between us.

- We can use the Triangle as a communication "traffic light" of sorts, helping us to know when it's best to *stop, wait, or go* when talking with our partners.

- Taking in good feelings can sometimes bring up painful feelings from the past. Allowing for both is healing.

- Emotionally opening up with our partners is a process. Over time, our capacity to be emotionally present with our partners will expand, and our fears will subside.

PART III:

Rewiring in Action

CHAPTER SEVEN

Feeling and Dealing

"Being deeply loved by someone gives you strength,
while loving someone deeply gives you courage."

Lao Tzu

The main goal that's brought us here is having better, more satisfying relationships. And the key to doing so lies in our capacity to be emotionally mindful. To be attuned to both ourselves and to our partners. To be able to manage and express our feelings while staying present, engaged, and responsive. To hang in when the going gets tough. And to see our way through to a better place. That's what helps us feel safe and secure in our relationships. That's what grows and strengthens our bonds. That's what deepens our love for each other.

These are the emotional capacities that people with a secure attachment style bring to their relationships. They're able to show up wholeheartedly and make good use of their feelings while staying connected and engaged with their partners. But it's not as though they possess some superhuman powers that the rest of us weren't fortunate enough to be endowed with. Remember, we're all born with the capacity to express our feelings, to connect emotionally with others, and to love and be loved. We come into the world ready to do all of these things.

The main difference is that some of us had early experiences in life that nurtured these capacities and supported our emotional development, and some of us did not. Those of us with an insecure attachment style had experiences that left us feeling afraid of truly expressing ourselves for fear of losing our most important relationships. In order to stay connected with our caregivers, we developed coping strategies to manage and in many instances suppress our core innate feelings. These strategies were once helpful to us but now thwart our emotional growth, and in turn impair our present-day relationships.

The good news is that while the opportunity to develop these emotional capacities to feel, deal, and relate may seem to have passed some of us by, they don't come with an expiration date. They don't fall into the "use it or lose it" category. They're still inside of us waiting to come out, ready to be called on and put to use. We just need to awaken them, nurture them, and strengthen them. If we're ready and willing, they're all there for the taking. The only thing keeping us from their benefits is a holdover from our early conditioning—fear.

Therein lies the essence of our work—to free ourselves from a fear that is no longer warranted and to reclaim our innate emotional capabilities. Unearth the aspects of our core self that have been buried and to reintegrate them into the totality of our being. Give our healthy strivings to express ourselves, however small or tentative they may be, a chance. Expand and strengthen our emotional repertoire so that we can bring our full and best self to our relationships. Become the people we were meant to be.

All of us can develop an earned secure attachment style by learning how to feel, deal, and relate mindfully in our relationships. Instead of letting our defenses lead the way, we can allow our core self to emerge and step forward. Instead of acting out our feelings, we can be open and direct. Instead of getting overwhelmed or shutting down, we can take risks and do things differently. We can find a way to show the sides of ourselves we once learned to hide. We can express what we really feel, need, and want, and be emotionally present for our partners. That's what it means to love like we mean it.

But doing so requires us to be able to differentiate our core emotions from our defenses and distress so that we can identify and work with our feelings and respond in an authentic and constructive way. One that's aligned with our true self and how we want to be in our relationships. One that will help us get to a better place with our partners. This is precisely what the work in the previous four chapters has helped us to do. Let's take a moment to review the four steps that got us to this point:

Step One: Recognize and Name—
Identifying when we've been triggered (when we've gotten activated and are responding defensively) and labeling it as such.

Step Two: Stop, Drop, and Stay—Slowing
down, focusing inward, and working through our emotional experience.

Step Three: Pause and Reflect—Stepping
back, making sense of our emotional experience, listening to what it's telling us, and deciding how best to respond.

Step Four: Mindfully Relate—
Thoughtfully expressing our core feelings, needs, and desires, and engaging with our partners in a constructive manner.

Separately each of these four steps addresses different aspects of our emotional experience. While they are arranged in a sequence that is designed to guide us through triggered moments in our lives, they also can be applied individually as needed. We can use them to navigate different aspects of our emotional lives.

For instance, at one point we might recognize that we're getting activated (e.g., our chest tightens) or responding defensively (e.g., our voice gets louder, or we start to check out), so we take a deep breath and calm ourselves and then attempt to reengage with our partners from a more receptive state. Here, we'd be drawing on the work of Step One ("Recognize and Name"). At another moment, we might realize that we're having some feelings and work to stay present with our emotional experience. This is the work of Step Two ("Stop, Drop, and Stay"). At a different point in time, we might find ourselves reflecting on an emotional experience that previously occurred and trying to make sense of it. Here, we'd be doing the work of Step Three ("Pause and Reflect"). Or as we're engaging with our partners, we might notice that we're getting ahead of ourselves, so we slow ourselves down and pay attention to what's happening between us. This would be the work of Step Four ("Mindfully Relate").

In each of these situations, we're making an effort to deal more mindfully with our emotional experience. Sometimes, that's all that's needed to keep us on track. We notice what's going on for us in the moment and do what we need to do. But sometimes, when our old programming kicks in, we need to draw upon all four steps and implement the whole sequence to navigate our way through our emotional experience and make the best of it, to help us identify the feelings, needs, or desires that we would typically leave out and find the courage to begin to share them.

Thus far in our journey together, we've examined each of the four steps in isolation. Now comes the time when we put them all together. In this chapter, we'll visit with three people, each with a different attachment style, and take a look at how they made use of the four steps in their lives. While each of their stories is different and unique to their lives, their experiences are universal and provide us with an opportunity to see how we might use the four steps ourselves.

Let's begin with Craig, who we first met in Chapter Two.

○   ○   ○

Finding the Courage to Feel

After being away for a week on a work trip, Craig settled into his seat for the flight home. During his time away he had ended up having more downtime than he had anticipated in which he found himself thinking a great deal about his relationship with Lydia, his fiancée. Craig felt sad about the difficulties that they'd been having and how his ambivalence about moving forward in their relationship had caused Lydia such pain. Being away afforded Craig some distance from which he saw more clearly how he'd been putting up barriers and keeping her at arm's length, and it bothered him.

Craig found himself missing Lydia, feeling loving feelings toward her, and wanting to reach out and be close to her. Feelings that seemed elusive when they were together but clearly existed inside of him. Craig wondered what would happen if he could show Lydia how he truly felt. If he could allow himself to be emotionally vulnerable and open with her. If he could express what was in his heart and tell Lydia how much she meant to him. If he could live from a more openhearted place instead of being constricted by fear. What would that be like? How might things be different for them? He wanted to find out, but the prospect of doing so felt scary to Craig.

If I can't make this work now, when will I? Craig thought to himself as the plane took off.

○   ○   ○

Becoming Aware

By the time Craig started therapy, his avoidant attachment style was deeply ingrained. It was a formidable outgrowth of being raised in a fractured and contentious family in which he learned to suppress his true feelings and deny his needs for closeness and connection in order to survive. His nervous system was governed by implicit programming that made closeness and connection feel threatening to him and led him to perceive his romantic partners as untrustworthy or inadequate, which kept him safe but alone. Craig was caught in patterns of responding that prevented him from having the kind of relationship that deep down he truly wanted.

The main issue for Craig was that he was unaware of why he was having such a hard time being successful in love. He had no idea that his perceptions and behaviors were being shaped by outdated internal working models from his distant past. As far as Craig was concerned, everything would be fine if Lydia would back off and stop giving him such a hard time. If she'd just give him some space, he'd come around. *Right?* Craig didn't realize that he was repeatedly getting triggered and responding defensively in his relationship as though he was somehow still in danger and needed to protect himself. He was unaware that his early programming was still steering his ship and fear was getting the best of him.

In order for Craig to be able to free himself from his early wiring and move forward in his relationship in a healthy, more integrated way, it was necessary for him to grow his emotional awareness and open up to his feelings. He needed to start working with the four steps.

The first order of business for Craig was to slow down and pay attention to what was happening for him so that he could begin to *recognize and name* when he'd gotten triggered. But slowing down was not something Craig was accustomed to doing. It's just not how he operated. Instead, Craig was used to acting on impulse, a behavior that often served him well in his work but was wreaking havoc in his love life. No sooner had one of his emotional hot buttons been pushed than his defenses were up and running. He'd start arguing with Lydia, questioning and challenging her, and defending his case. Or he'd get caught in a spiral of negative thoughts—doubting Lydia's trustworthiness, questioning her intellect, seeing her behavior as needy and unappealing—and end up pulling away or shutting down.

As hard as Craig tried to put the brakes on when interacting with Lydia, he'd get so caught up in the heat of the moment that it would get away from him, and he'd lose track of himself. In order to be able to slow down and observe himself in real time, Craig needed to spend some time building his emotional mindfulness skills when he wasn't feeling so reactive. He needed to strike while the iron was cold, not hot. By doing so, he could work at strengthening the downward connections between his higher and lower brain, between his prefrontal cortex and his amygdala in particular, so that he could better manage his threat response when it became activated.

So when Craig would come in for his therapy session, we would engage in an emotion-focused version of Monday morning quarterbacking. Craig would recount a charged episode he had with Lydia, while pausing frequently to take a look at what was emotionally going on inside of him. As Craig put his defenses aside and tuned into his felt experience, he was surprised by what he discovered going on in his body—his chest would tighten, his heart rate would speed up, and his stomach became constricted, all of which are classic signs of anxiety. He hadn't realized that his nervous system had gotten activated which prompted him to respond in a defensive manner. But by slowing down the action and creating some room, and with an assist from the Triangle of Experience that you learned about in Chapter Three, Craig began to tease apart the different elements of his emotional experience—his feelings, anxiety, and defenses—and make some sense of what was happening for him.

Next Craig needed to deal with what was causing him to get triggered. He needed to *stop, drop, and stay* present to the emotions that were stirring under the surface. This step was also challenging for Craig, as it can be for any of us who are accustomed to avoiding our feelings. His old inclination to clamp down on his feelings was strong. But with some encouragement and support, he began to lean into his emotional experience and over time discovered a number of feelings he hadn't known were at hand for him. In particular his vulnerability, sadness, love, and longing to be close. The feelings and needs that he had long ago learned to deny. The feelings he needed to befriend and reclaim in order to reconnect to his true self.

As Craig worked at staying with his feelings, as he breathed into them and moved through them, the origins of his old fear of being emotionally open with others came into view. Various memories from his childhood that depicted the unrelenting pressure he had felt as a little boy bubbled to the surface.

Everybody in young Craig's world (his mother, father, and sister) seemed to want something from him. Everybody had their own agenda. No one seemed interested in his feelings or needs. No one seemed to be there just for him. Longing for love from both of his parents, longing to be seen, heard, and valued, Craig got caught in the middle of their fraught relationship dynamics. When he got closer to his mother, he sensed his father's frustration and disapproval, and when he sought his father's attention and engagement, he felt his mother's sadness and dismay as well as his sister's disdain. Craig felt trapped and powerless, unable to show his feelings without experiencing some kind of recrimination or potential fallout. It was all too much for a little boy. What was he to do? How was he to survive? Not surprisingly, Craig learned to bury his feelings and put away his needs for love and connection. He closed off his heart to avoid the pain that inevitably came with needing others. He vowed to go it alone and never rely on anyone ever again.

And here he was, many years later, unknowingly still doing the same thing.

As Craig worked through the mix of feelings inside of him, he began to make sense of the emotional dynamics that had been at play for him. By *pausing and reflecting*, he saw how his arguing and distrust were caused by an old fear of being emotionally present with others, one that he now understood could be traced back to his early experience in his family. His past was intruding on his present and coloring his relationship with Lydia. No wonder closeness and connection felt so threatening to him. Somewhere inside of him was a little boy longing for love but frightened of the consequences of allowing himself to need anyone else or letting them become important to him.

While Craig's understanding of his emotional dynamics and his ability to observe and stay present with his feelings were growing, and while he had begun to share what he was learning about himself with Lydia, he still found it challenging to get beyond Step One when he was interacting with her. When he was by himself, Craig was able to calm his distress and begin to sort out the tangle of feelings inside of him. But when he was with Lydia, his old programming proved to be a force to be reckoned with. He often felt helpless to its sway and had a hard time reining himself in and trying something different. Afterward, when the dust had settled, Craig was full of remorse and felt ashamed that his defenses had gotten the best of him. He wondered if he might be too far gone to ever turn things around, do things differently, and be successful in a relationship. Still, to Craig's credit, he kept getting back up on the horse and giving it another try.

Eventually Craig's hard work, persistence, and commitment paid off, and things started to shift.

○ ○ ○

Coming Home to Love

As Craig lay in bed waiting for Lydia to join him, he thought about how it felt to be home. He was happy to see Lydia, and she seemed to feel the same way. The tension between them that had been in the air before he left on his work trip seemed to have evaporated, and while a little tentative, they were both making an effort to put their best foot forward. Craig had gotten Lydia some flowers, and she had prepared a special dinner for them. It felt good to unwind together and reconnect.

Craig glanced over toward the bathroom and could see Lydia's reflection in the mirror. Their eyes met, and she smiled at him. Craig felt warm inside as they looked at each other. He could see the desire in her face. He could tell that she wanted to be with him, to make love. After all, it had been a while since they were last together in that way. Craig wanted to as well. Didn't he?

Then, almost imperceptibly, Craig's chest tightened. Craig rolled over in bed and faced the other way. He felt anxious and uncomfortable. *But how do you know she's for real?* he asked himself. *How do you know she's not just being nice so you'll marry her? I mean, how can you be sure?*

His agitation rising, Craig sat up on the edge of the bed, leaned forward, and put his hands on his knees. Then it hit him. He recognized what was up. *It's happening again,* Craig said to himself. *This is it. This is how that old fear shows up. I start to open up, and I get afraid.* Craig put his hand on his chest, took a breath and let it out slowly. And then again. And again. He shifted his feet on the floor and tried to feel grounded. As his nerves settled a bit, Craig tried to reconnect with the loving feelings that were there almost a moment ago. The feelings that he now understood were making him uncomfortable. The feelings he wanted to be able to share.

Just then, Craig heard Lydia walk into the room. He felt the impulse to get up and busy himself, but he resisted. Instead, he sat motionless staring at the floor.

Sensing that something was up, Lydia sat down next to Craig and put her hand on his back. "Hon, what's the matter?" she asked tentatively. "Are you okay?"

Craig opened his mouth to speak and then paused. He felt anxious and unsure of himself. He wondered what he should do. What he should say. *Just tell her the truth,* he thought, and then gave himself a little push.

"Um, this is hard to tell you," he said. "I mean, I was lying here thinking about you, about how good it is to see you, about how nice it feels to be together. And then I started to get worried. Like something bad is going to happen. Like it's dangerous for me to let myself be open. I got anxious and started to close up. But I don't want to. I don't want to close up. I mean, I love you so much. I want to be with you. But I guess I get afraid."

Craig had been staring at the floor the whole time he was speaking. He had felt too vulnerable to look at Lydia. But he found the courage to steal a glance in Lydia's direction and was relieved to see a look of tenderness in her eyes. They sat quietly for a moment, looking at each other, and then Lydia responded.

"I'm glad you're telling me and not keeping it to yourself," she said. "It feels so much better to know what's going on with you. To know what's going on inside of you. I get it. I get why it's scary. You've been hurt. But it's okay. You're okay. We're going to be okay."

Craig put his arms around Lydia and pulled her close. It felt good.

○   ○   ○

This was a breakthrough moment for Craig. All the work that he'd been doing to grow his emotional mindfulness skills came to bear. He used the four steps in real time to break the cycle of his old programming, push through his fears, and try something different. He recognized he'd gotten triggered, calmed himself, tapped into his feelings, and mindfully shared them with Lydia. He opened his heart, shared what was going on for him, and let his love come through.

That's a huge step for someone who had kept his heart under wraps for over forty years. It's a huge step for any of us with an avoidant attachment style—to open up to our feelings, allow ourselves to be vulnerable, and share our feelings with others. But it's precisely what is needed for us to be able to turn things around in our relationships.

Of course, Craig is not home free. There will surely be challenging moments for him to come. While Lydia responded positively to his opening up, that may not always be the case. At times she may get defensive, and so may Craig. Their old wiring will get the best of them and take over. That's to be expected. It takes time to develop new patterns of responding. Craig will need to keep at it and work through the four steps with every opportunity that presents itself.

Speaking of which, Craig should be on the lookout for any residual fear that might show up after he's allowed himself to be vulnerable and open with Lydia. That's to be expected as well. When we open ourselves up to greater intimacy with our partners, especially if we tend to be more avoidant, it's not uncommon to experience a bit of anxiety afterward. We stretch a little and then start to feel anxious as if we went too far and then feel inclined to withdraw or retreat. But it's not a sign of danger. It's just an echo from our implicit memory reverberating in our nervous system. So if we can anticipate that this kind of thing may happen, we can "name it to tame it" when it does and not be thrown. We can say, "Ah! There's my old fear. I did something outside of my comfort zone, and it's acting up." It's a sign that we're breaking new ground. That we're on the right track.

As we can see with Craig, developing our emotional mindfulness skills takes time. But with each effort we make to attend to our experience in an intentional way, we strengthen our abilities. Little by little over time, it all adds up. And then all of a sudden something clicks, and the work we've been doing comes together. We're able to see what's happening in the moment and shift gears. We're able to do things differently and get somewhere better.

To that end, let's now look at how Arlene, a client of mine in her early forties with a fearful-avoidant attachment style, made use of the four steps.

○　○　○

Finding the "I" in the Storm

Arlene had been out of sorts all morning. She kept seeing Mitch's angry face in her mind's eye and hearing him go off on a rant. Arlene had tried to talk to him the night before about scheduling a childbirth class at the nearby hospital. Their baby would be here in just a couple of months and they were running out of time. Given how exhausted Arlene had been lately, it felt more manageable for her to take a class that was offered over the course of a few different evenings. But Mitch didn't like that idea at all and for some reason ended up pitching a fit, arguing that he needed time to unwind after work. Arlene was so shaken by his extreme response that she ended up agreeing to attend a daylong course on the weekend that would be physically excruciating and practically impossible for her.

Feeling upset, Arlene paced around the house. She kept vacillating between two extremes—wanting to lay into Mitch for being "a selfish child" and feeling helpless and distraught. While not an unfamiliar experience for Arlene, it had been quite a while since she had felt so emotionally pulled about. All the work she had done in therapy, combined with several years of being in recovery and a daily meditation practice, had helped her to manage her emotions better, unlike the past, when they could feel overwhelming and get away from her.

But lately, plagued by months of morning sickness that wouldn't let up; she'd been feeling emotionally raw and on edge. *Maybe that's why I'm feeling so upset?* Arlene wondered. *Or is something else going on?* She thought about it for a moment and then realized what she needed to do. She needed to get to the bottom of what had gotten stirred up for her and to find some clarity. She needed to draw on the work that she'd been doing in her therapy and work through the four steps.

Arlene sat down on the couch and sighed as she tried to get comfortable. She put both feet on the floor and rested her hands on her lap, noting how the fabric of her pants felt against her palms. Doing so helped her feel a bit grounded. Then Arlene closed her eyes, focused inside, and pictured the episode from the night before. As she replayed the experience in her mind, she noticed her throat getting constricted and her chest tightening—the activation of her nervous system was becoming apparent.

Arlene breathed into the tension inside of her and tried to open up and stay present to whatever was coming up. As she sensed into her felt experience more deeply she recognized what it was and named it. *Fear*, she said to herself. *I'm feeling afraid.* That seemed to help. *But what's so scary?* Arlene wondered. She started to think about what might be making her feel afraid but then stopped herself, not wanting to get lost in her thoughts. She knew from past experience that's not where the answer would be found. Instead she focused on her feelings and tried to stay open to what she might discover.

Suddenly Arlene saw herself as a child, helplessly watching an all too familiar scene: her parents arguing, their voices getting louder, the tension mounting, and then her father snapping and becoming violent. She watched in horror as he picked up a vase and smashed it on the floor. Her child-self stood frozen in fear, feeling powerless and alone.

Arlene began to cry, wave after wave of sadness and pain rolling through her. She felt as though she might be overcome by her feelings but told herself to "just breathe," knowing from experience that if she stayed with her emotions and saw them through, eventually the storm would subside as it always does, no matter how powerful the waves of emotion. Arlene was right. It did. Once the waters calmed, Arlene found herself feeling for her younger self. For the frightened child inside her who had been stuck in this awful memory and needed to know it was over. Drawing on the work she'd done in therapy, Arlene imagined going to her child-self, picking her up, rubbing her back and consoling her—reassuring her that she's okay, that she's safe now, and that she's not alone.

As the child inside of her relaxed, so did Arlene. She took a deep breath to take in the sense of relief that had come over her. But, as she did, Arlene noticed something else now stirring in her. Another feeling was emerging. Her jaw had tightened, and energy was rising inside of her. Arlene recognized that she was feeling angry. A feeling that she had learned to clamp down on and hold inside. A feeling that had once felt too dangerous to express. But it was a feeling that she knew she needed to honor and learn to abide with. A feeling she needed to reclaim in order to be able to stand her ground when needed. This was one of those times. *How dare they behave that way in front of their kids!* Arlene thought to herself as she leaned into her anger toward her parents and gave it room. *What the hell were they thinking? That was just so wrong!*

As Arlene allowed herself to feel the force of her anger move through her and eventually dissipate, something inside of her shifted. She noticed that she no longer felt small, like a child. Instead, she felt emboldened, more embodied, and more adult. The past was receding, and Arlene was coming more fully into the present moment.

No wonder I've been so upset, Arlene thought to herself. *I got triggered.* As she reflected on what she encountered inside of herself, she could see how the trauma of her past had impacted her recent experience with Mitch. His angry behavior had activated old memories that reverberated throughout her nervous system. As a result, she had felt frightened, powerless, and without options. Just like her child-self had surely felt all those years ago.

What's more, while Mitch's anger scared Arlene, so did her own. Her early experience in life, in which anger became equated with violence and destruction, had led her to avoid anger at all costs. Arlene unknowingly defended against feeling or directly expressing her anger for fear that it would destroy her relationships. Consequently she remained trapped by her childhood fear and deprived of the clarity and direction that healthy anger could afford her in her adult life. She was unable to feel as though her needs were important, to advocate for herself, to set limits, and to have healthy boundaries.

Had Arlene been free to feel and make use of her anger, she might have called Mitch on his reaction in the moment and told him that his behavior was not acceptable. Or at the very least, she might have paused the conversation and suggested to Mitch that they could talk later when he calmed down. But through the eyes of her child-self, Arlene had felt afraid, helpless, and without options.

As the pieces fell into place for her, Arlene thought about what she should do. No longer activated, and feeling more aligned with her adult self, she could see Mitch more objectively. While his reaction was certainly over the top, she knew he wasn't dangerous. *Maybe he was also feeling stressed and emotionally depleted?* Arlene considered. *Maybe he had gotten triggered as well? Maybe he'd be less defensive now that he's calmed down.* More solidly in her adult self, Arlene could see that she was not without options. She could find a way to talk to Mitch and tell him how she felt. She could try to engage in a discussion that could possibly get them to a better place.

Of course, the prospect of opening up and being direct about her feelings made Arlene nervous. Her old programming was still in need of an update. In order for that to happen, she would need to face her fears and be honest with Mitch. She would need to let him know what she was feeling and what she needed from him. At the very least she would need to give expressing her feelings a try in order to see what was possible.

That night, after Mitch had gotten home from work, Arlene shored up her courage and asked him if they could talk about what had happened the night before. Feeling a bit shaky inside, she took her time and spoke slowly, trying to stay centered. Mitch initially seemed on edge, but when Arlene told him that his reaction was triggering for her and why, he softened and eventually apologized. Mitch acknowledged that he had been feeling pretty stressed out after a hard day at work and had lost it. But regardless of what was going on for him, he wasn't trying to make an excuse. Mitch felt awful about how he'd behaved and told Arlene that he would never want to act in a way that would make her feel afraid.

Feeling safe to continue, Arlene took another step forward and explained to Mitch how she had only agreed to go to the daylong childbirth class because she'd gotten scared. It was also hard for her to honor her own needs as important and worthy of consideration. She didn't want to do that anymore. Arlene explained that she was too uncomfortable and exhausted to get through a daylong class and actually get something out of it. And she wanted it to be a positive experience for them. She needed Mitch to understand how hard it would be for her and told him she couldn't do it. They'd need to figure something else out.

Arlene could see that Mitch was disappointed, but he acquiesced without any pushback. Gone was the conflict and discord of the day before. He didn't reject her. Instead he respected her needs. Something about the way in which she approached him, the way in which he responded, and the way in which they were being with each other was allowing for a new experience.

○   ○   ○

Showing up in this way with Mitch was new for Arlene. Given her long-standing fear of getting hurt or being rejected by others, she had a hard time owning and communicating her anger and directly addressing conflict. It had just felt too threatening to her. But by using the four steps, she was able to modulate and work through the mix of feelings inside of her and assert her truth. She found the courage to lean in and express herself in a healthy way.

But reclaiming her anger and adaptively asserting herself was only one of the growing edges that Arlene would need to address if she wanted to free herself from the confines of her early programming. Equally as threatening to her was the prospect of being emotionally vulnerable with Mitch, of letting her guard down and allowing him to get close to her, of being willing to depend on him to be there for her.

As is common for those of us with a fearful-avoidant attachment style, Arlene both longed for emotional closeness *and* was terrified of it. She had long been caught in a "come here-go away" interpersonal dynamic in which she would seek out love and connection, but when anyone would try to get close to her, she'd push them away or withdraw in fear. Not surprisingly her relationships had been characterized by emotional unpredictability and chaos, similar to what she experienced as a child in her family. While her relationship with Mitch was much more stable, Arlene's early wiring persisted, and despite often feeling lonely and longing for a deeper connection with Mitch, she could still put up barriers to emotional intimacy. For Arlene to have a stable and fulfilling relationship, she would need to honor her needs for connection. She would have to reclaim her innate attachment needs and allow herself to be open to love.

Of course, the opportunity for Arlene to do just that was right around the corner.

○   ○   ○

Befriending the Softer Side

Arlene was relieved that she and Mitch had finally made some time to work on the baby's room. She was sorting through a pile of baby clothes and figuring out where to put them while Mitch was taking apart his computer setup to move it elsewhere. As Mitch sat on the floor wrapping cords around different components, he started to share what was on his mind.

"Well, there's certainly not going to be much time for gaming when the baby comes. That's for sure. Pretty much no downtime for either of us," he said, sounding wistful. "Our whole world is about to get completely turned upside down. Kind of freaks me out."

This was different for Mitch. He wasn't one to open up and talk about his feelings. By doing so, Mitch was making a bid for connection with Arlene. He was reaching out, sharing his fears, and trying to navigate this life-changing event together. Had Arlene not had her back to Mitch, maybe that would have been more apparent to her. But instead of engaging in a conversation, she flew off the handle. Arlene turned around to face Mitch and blurted out, "Well, you're going to have to figure out that one on your own! I can't be taking care of a baby *and* you!"

Mitch looked startled. "Wow! That was harsh," he said, and hurriedly proceeded to gather the rest of his things. As he stood up to leave, he looked over at Arlene and said, "I just can't win with you!" and walked off in a huff.

Arlene was going to go after him but stopped herself. She was feeling too charged up and didn't want to get into it. Besides, she knew where that would go. *Fine. Let him stew about it,* she thought to herself, trying to shrug it off. *I really don't care!*

Arlene went back to putting the baby's things away. As she focused on what she was doing and began to calm down a bit, she noticed something niggling at her insides. She kept seeing the hurt expression on Mitch's face when he turned to leave. *I guess I was kind of harsh,* she thought to herself, feeling badly. Then she wondered, *Why did I have such a strong reaction?*

Arlene sat down, focused inward, and tried to sense what was going on for her emotionally. She thought about what Mitch had tried to say to her, but this time instead of feeling annoyed with him, she noticed that she felt anxious. Her body was tense. It occurred to her that Mitch was being vulnerable with her. He was reaching out and trying to connect, and it made her uncomfortable. Just as her own vulnerability made her uncomfortable. She couldn't tolerate it in herself, and she was realizing she couldn't tolerate it in him. At least that's how her nervous system had responded.

Arlene felt a wave of guilt and started to cry. She could see what was going on for her. Old fears had gotten activated. Her childhood fears of being vulnerable and needing someone—fears of letting anyone close, letting anyone *matter*—were again in her current life. But now instead of wanting to lash out or run as she had in the past, it pained her.

That's not who I want to be, Arlene thought to herself. *I don't want to push Mitch away. I want to be able to be there for him. I want to let him be there for me. I want to be okay with that.*

As Arlene began to feel clearer and more centered, she made her way to the garage where she found Mitch setting up his computer. She wanted to talk. She wanted to repair things between them and try again.

"Mitch?" she said.

"What?" Mitch responded, with an edge in his voice.

Arlene could tell he was still smarting. She felt herself tense up slightly in response but took a breath and told herself to take it slow. She wanted to talk with Mitch in a caring way. She wanted Mitch to be able to hear her. She wanted to get through.

"Um, I'm sorry I lashed out," she said, tentatively. "You were trying to talk about how you're feeling and I shut the conversation down."

"Yeah. Well it feels pretty awful," Mitch responded.

"I'm sure," Arlene said, feeling badly. "I'm sorry for that."

"I just don't know how to be around you," Mitch added, shaking his head.

"You were being fine. I'm the one who got uncomfortable. You were reaching out, trying to connect, and I guess I got anxious. I don't know. It's like I can't tolerate feeling vulnerable. Like it feels threatening to me in some way, and my walls go up."

"Why?" Mitch asked, the edge in his voice starting to fade.

"It's kind of like a reflex. It wasn't safe to be vulnerable in my family. My parents were too wrapped up in their shit. It's like a young part of me gets afraid that something bad is going to happen and I lash out. But I *do* need you. I love you. I want to be there for you. I want to be able to connect in that way. It feels scary, but I want to try."

Arlene looked in Mitch's eyes. She could see that he had softened. She could see that she was getting through. She could feel her love for Mitch. She could feel his care for her. It didn't scare her. It felt right.

O O O

For those of us with a fearful-avoidant attachment style, the intensity of our feelings can pull us in opposing directions and cause us to lose our center and sense of self. In particular, both our attachment needs for closeness and independence can feel dangerous and overwhelm us. Fearing hurt or rejection, and without a reliable strategy to constructively deal with our feelings, we get tossed about, unable to move comfortably toward intimacy or assertively deal with conflict and difference.

But secure relationships require that we are able to do both. We need to be able to calm the distress we feel inside and manage our emotions so that we can hear, honor, and allow for both sides of our experience. Ultimately, we need to be able to let others in, *and* we need to be able to assert our boundaries in a healthy way. Arlene used the four steps to do just that.

In both instances with Mitch, Arlene recognized that there was something more going on emotionally beneath her surface reactivity that needed to be addressed. By going inward and attending to her emotional experience, she was able to disentangle her child-self from her adult-self and find her way more solidly into the present moment. She was able to hear her truth and follow its lead, then by taking a risk both to assert her limits with Mitch *and* be vulnerable and connect with him more deeply, she is coming to see that the dangers she anticipated no longer exist. Using the four steps to guide her, Arlene is learning that she can safely open up to a wider range of emotional choices and a more integrated way of being in her relationship.

On that note, let's take a look at how someone with an anxious attachment style makes use of the four steps.

○   ○   ○

Finding the Courage to Deal

When Troy first started to work the four steps, it was difficult for him to hear and trust his core feelings. For as far back as he could remember, the buzz of his anxiety was omnipresent, clouding his judgment. A graduate student in his mid-twenties, he had a hard time being emotionally present in his relationships, often second-guessed himself, and worried that there was something wrong with him.

Adopted at birth and raised by parents who had a fair amount of anxiety and conflict around emotion, Troy grew up with a chronic sense of uncertainty, unsure that his parents would be there if he needed them and afraid that he would do or say something that would disappoint or upset them, be too much in some way and get rejected. As a child, Troy had a recurring nightmare in which he desperately tried to catch up to his parents as he followed them down the twisted hallways of a strange building. At some point inevitably his parents would turn a corner, and when Troy did as well a few steps later, they'd be gone. Nowhere to be found. Surely, little Troy felt as though he had done something to drive them away.

This chronic sense of insecurity followed Troy into his adult relationships in which he found himself with romantic partners who were emotionally unpredictable and unable to show up in a way that felt satisfying to him. In addition, Troy was acutely sensitive to any sign of possible disconnection or discord and often worried that he had done something to screw things up. If Troy was going to have a healthy relationship, he would need to disentangle himself from his early wiring and be able to trust and make better use of his emotions with his partners. In particular, he needed to be mindful of his needs for connection and reassurance, and to express them in a healthy way.

Troy met Andre at an opportune time in his emotional journey. Through his work in therapy, Troy was beginning to emerge from the fog of his anxiety and more readily connect with his core feelings. Of course, the challenge Troy now faced was for him to be able to do this while in a relationship.

A few years older than Troy, Andre seemed more emotionally mature than Troy's previous partners. From the beginning, something clicked and felt right to both of them. Aloft on a billowy cloud of new love, the early days of their relationship were characterized by a warmth and caring that felt wonderful and new to them both. But gradually, Troy's anxiety started to creep onto the scene. He found himself feeling increasingly on edge and worrying that disaster was just around the corner. His old programming was making itself known.

Hearing and Honoring What's Inside

Troy started to feel anxious as he and Andre walked up the steps to the restaurant. They were attending a party to celebrate the birthday of an old friend of Andre's and there would be over a hundred people in attendance. He would be meeting friends and associates of Andre's for the first time and wanted to make a good impression. But as they mingled with the other guests and people were warm and friendly, the tension he initially felt subsided. By the time they made their way to their assigned table for dinner, Troy felt pretty relaxed.

Troy and Andre sat down next to each other and chatted a bit before people began to stand and say a few words about the mutual friend whose birthday they had gathered to celebrate. After one particular toast that was funny and had everyone laughing, Troy commented to Andre that it was nice to see the guest of honor smiling and having a good time, given how depressed he always seemed.

Troy assumed Andre would simply agree with him, but saw rather quickly that the comment rubbed Andre the wrong way.

Looking serious, Andre leaned in and said under his breath, "Yeah, that's true. But it feels kind of impolite to be talking about him like that at his birthday party. Don't you think?"

Troy thought about it for a moment and then said, "Oh, you're right. I'm sorry. That was thoughtless of me."

"It's okay," Andre replied. He smiled at Troy and then focused back on the proceedings, seeming to have let it go.

But had he? Troy wasn't so sure. He kept looking at Andre to see if he was really okay but couldn't tell. Troy started to feel anxious and began to worry that Andre might be angry with him and that something bad might happen. Throughout dinner, Troy kept trying to get Andre's attention, hoping for a reassuring glance or comment that might ease his nervousness, but Andre was engrossed in the conversation at the table and didn't seem to notice.

Troy told himself that he was being silly and tried to put the whole thing out of his mind. But he couldn't. As he watched Andre engaging with other people and having a good time, his nervousness grew. Then Troy started to feel angry. He didn't have to come to this dinner. He did it for Andre. *He's such a jerk!* Troy thought to himself. *It was a harmless comment. I didn't mean anything by it. Besides, that guy is depressed!* And then a fatalistic thought: *This relationship is never going to work. We're just too different. I need to cut my losses and move on. Get out before it gets too serious.*

Troy excused himself from the table and stepped outside "to get some fresh air." He was hoping Andre would notice he was upset and come after him. But as he walked around the block, he recognized what was going on for him. He was going to an extreme place in his head—his anxiety had gotten the best of him and he was becoming defensive. Troy took a deep breath, pursed his lips, and let it out slowly. He realized he needed to calm down or he might do something rash.

It took a little work, but as Troy's nerves began to settle he saw more clearly what was going on. His old attachment fears had gotten activated. Troy had just been talking in therapy about how this can happen and here it was staring him in the face, live and in person. Troy realized that he was feeling with Andre the same way he had felt as a child, worried that he'd done something to push his unpredictable mother over the edge and that she'd blow up and withdraw. He flashed back to the time when he went to his parents' bedroom in the middle of the night feeling afraid, and his mother lost it and screamed at him. And here he was not only worried that he might have done something to put his relationship with Andre in jeopardy but also afraid to reach out for reassurance, afraid that Andre would perceive him as needy and get upset with him.

Troy sat down on a bench and put his hand on his chest. He felt compassion for the frightened child inside of him and imagined comforting and consoling him. As the tension in him subsided, and he began to feel more grounded, Troy saw more clearly how he had gotten caught up in a swirl of distress, that he'd gone to a hopeless place and that his thinking had become extreme. It was likely the same thing that would happen when he was a child.

Andre is not my mother, he told himself. *He's not a jerk. He just had a reaction. I can make a mistake. It doesn't make me a bad person. It doesn't mean that our relationship is over.* Hearing the reassuring voice of his adult-self helped, but Troy still felt unsettled. He knew that it wasn't going to be enough to dispel his fears. He was still worried about how Andre might respond should he share his fears with him. He would need to find a way to open up to Andre and see what was possible.

Later in the car on their way home, Troy mustered up the courage to ask Andre if they could talk about what happened at dinner. "You know, I said I was sorry for the comment I made, but it seemed like you were still upset with me."

Initially, Andre said that he wasn't, that he had let it go. To his mind he had told Troy how he felt and that was that. But as they talked about it further, Andre confessed that he might have continued to feel bothered. They'd been sitting with a few people whom Andre didn't know well and he was afraid they overheard the exchange.

"But, I'm over it now," he said to Troy with a smile. "No hard feelings."

Troy sighed. It felt better to talk. Finally, he could let it go. Well, at least for the moment.

Later that evening, while they got ready for bed, Troy found himself feeling uneasy. He still felt as though something wasn't right between the two of them. While Andre had told Troy they were fine, his body language seemed to say something else. It was a long ride home after the party, and Andre wasn't his usual affectionate self. At the very least, they might have held hands at some point.

Troy tried telling himself that they were both tired, and he shouldn't worry about it; but his nervous system wasn't convinced. He knew he should probably talk about it further with Andre but worried that he might push him over the edge. *He's going to think I'm crazy,* Troy thought, but realized he had to see it through and find out.

Troy slowly walked into the bedroom and sat down on the bed, across from Andre. "You know," he said, feeling anxious, "I'm afraid that I'm going to sound neurotic, and I know that you said that everything is okay between us, but, it just seems as though you've been kind of distant. I mean, we usually hold hands in the car, and you haven't touched me at all since we've gotten home."

Andre looked exasperated and said, "Yeah, well, you haven't been affectionate either."

"That's true," Troy admitted. "Um . . . I think I've been feeling kind of apprehensive. I mean, I know how you sometimes need space, and I didn't want to push it."

Andre looked down and was quiet for a moment. Then he looked up at Troy and said, "I guess I have been a bit restrained. I know I can do that sometimes. But I really wasn't aware that was happening. I'm sorry."

Troy could see the vulnerability in Andre's eyes. He reached out and touched his hand. "Can you just hold me?" Troy asked.

Andre leaned forward and put his arms around Troy. The warmth between them becoming palpable. It felt better. They'd found their way back to good.

○   ○   ○

From the outside looking in, it may seem absurd that Troy had such a strong reaction to Andre's disapproving response. But that's how it can go for those of us with an anxious attachment style. Any sign of discontent in our partners, no matter how subtle it may be, can be cause for alarm. Our amygdala reads it as a threat and sends out the troops. We get lost in a swirl of worry and fear that's impervious to rational thinking. It's only when we find a way to dial down our reactivity that we can see more clearly what's going on for us.

Often, calming ourselves is half the battle. But it's not enough. We need to be able to hear and honor our core feelings, needs, and desires and find the courage to communicate them directly to our partners. That's the only way we can disconfirm our fear-based expectations that our partners will respond badly, and our relationships will fall apart should we open up and express our true feelings.

Which was precisely what Troy used the four steps to do. By recognizing that he was feeling defensive and attending to his inner turmoil, Troy was able to see that he had gotten triggered. Internally, he was feeling vulnerable and in need of reassurance from Andre that they were okay, but Troy was afraid to reach out. By finding the courage to lean in and directly express his feelings, and by hanging in there and working things through to completion, Troy did the emotional work needed to begin to dispel his old fears and feel more secure in his relationship with Andre.

To his credit, Andre worked at it too. He was reflective, able to own his part in the matter and acknowledge what was going on for him, and showed up wholeheartedly as well. Both of them engaged in a process that enhanced the security of their connection. And it was a good thing, given that they were about to face a more difficult relationship challenge when Troy decided to accept a yearlong postgraduate fellowship in a city other than where they lived.

Given Troy's attachment history, this was a hard decision for him to make. As he considered his different options, Troy had to do a lot of work to separate out his old fear of doing something that would disappoint or upset others from his true feelings, in order to hear what he really wanted. When the offer came from this particular program, he knew it was where he wanted to go, but he worried about how Andre would react and what would happen.

Understandably, Andre was upset when Troy told him of his decision. Their relationship was still new, and he worried about how they would weather the separation and what it would mean for them in the long run. But they both were committed to each other and wanted to try to make it work.

In the days that followed, Troy couldn't help but notice how Andre would get sullen whenever friends would congratulate Troy on his news. It bothered him. He wanted Andre to put his own feelings aside and be happy for him. After all, they still had six months before Troy needed to leave. But when he told a friend how he was feeling, his frustration softened.

"Of course Andre is upset," his friend said to him. "He doesn't want you to go away. He loves you!" Troy felt embarrassed. His own discomfort had obscured the reason for Andre's sadness. *Why couldn't I see that?* Troy thought to himself. Good question.

That evening as Troy and Andre were lying on the couch together, Andre said to him, "You know, it's going to be really hard for me when you leave."

Troy felt uneasy. With a forced smile, he said, "Well, I'm here now!"

Andre was quiet for a moment and then said, half-heartedly, "Yeah, I know."

But Troy could see the sadness in Andre's eyes. He felt uncomfortable and looked away. Troy recognized feeling tense and focused inward. *I'm feeling guilty,* he quickly realized. *Like I'm doing something wrong. I'm afraid Andre's upset with me and I'm in trouble, like everything is going to fall apart and that will be the end of our relationship.*

Troy looked back at Andre. He felt for him. "I'm sorry," Troy said. "That was insensitive of me. I can see that you're sad, and I guess I get uncomfortable. I feel guilty, like I'm doing something wrong. Like a part of me is scared that you're upset with me, and you're going to bail."

Andre nodded with understanding and said, "I'm not upset with you. You're not doing anything wrong, and I'm not going to bail. I'm just sad. It's going to be hard. I love you."

"I love you too," Troy said with tears in his eyes. "It *is* going to be hard." He pulled Andre near him and held him close and then said, reassuringly, "I want to make this work. I know we can figure it out."

O   O   O

By working through the four steps, Troy's ability to recognize when he's been triggered and to attend to his emotional experience has gotten stronger. Here, he catches himself in real time, is mindful of his internal process, and leans in with Andre in an emotionally revealing way. In the past, when his threat alarm would go off, Troy might have held fast to his defenses and gotten caught up in a pointless argument. Instead, he stretches into a new way of being and opens himself up to receive Andre's love.

As Troy is learning, when we are mindful of our emotional experience, we discover how our defenses not only prevent something inside of us from being revealed, but they also thwart our ability to take in the good that comes our way. We may long for love, but what happens when it shows up? Do we welcome it with open arms, or does fear get in the way? For Troy it was the latter.

Through the lens of his internal working models, Troy unknowingly saw himself as the cause of Andre's distress. It made him feel guilty and at risk. In turn, he responded defensively by minimizing Andre's feelings and trying to make it all go away. Imagine if his process had stopped there. Look at what he would have missed out on. Receiving the very thing that would help him feel more solidly connected in his relationship—Andre's love.

When we do the work to attend to the underlying forces that can unconsciously control our behavior, we free ourselves up to have new experiences. Experiences that have the power to heal our inner wounds. Experiences that widen our hearts and deepen our connections with our loved ones. Experiences that change us and our relationships for the better.

The Way Forward

Craig, Arlene, and Troy are all engaged in a process of transformation. They're disentangling themselves from their early programming and reclaiming aspects of their emotional experience that had once been unavailable to them, hidden behind walls of fear. Each is restoring his or her capacity to be a fully functioning human being, becoming someone who is in touch with a full range of emotions and able to use them to good effect. Someone who is able to feel and deal while engaging with his or her partner. By showing up wholeheartedly to their relationship, they are maximizing its capacity to flourish.

That's what can happen when we work through the four steps. We can overcome our fears and free ourselves from the constriction of the past. We can move our attachment styles in the direction of earned security and get to a better place with our partners.

But as you can see, growing our emotional mindfulness skills takes work and time. It's definitely not something that happens overnight. Just like a ballerina spends hours at the barre, practicing and strengthening the movements that will one day enable her to perform a series of graceful, seemingly weightless leaps across the floor, so too is the work of strengthening the brain functions that over time will enable us to respond in a more mindful way in our relationships and bring our best self to the dance of love.

Each of us is in a different place on our emotional journey. Each of us has different strengths and areas for growth. Some of us might need to spend more time doing the work required of one step than another. Sometimes we may need to back up and do the work of a previous step, especially when our emotional experience doesn't shift. That's when there's more inside of us that we need to get to know, understand, and work with before we can move forward. But all that matters is that we keep coming back to our emotional experience, noticing where we are in the present moment, become attuned to what's going on inside of us, and do our best to stay engaged.

Of course, taking the risk to be emotionally open with our partners only gets us part of the way. We're going to need to hang in and find a way to work things through. But by showing up in an openhearted way, we're shifting our relationship dynamics. We're creating the possibility for something different. Sometimes that's just the beginning of a longer road. Sometimes it doesn't work out as we hoped it would. Sometimes our partners aren't able to join us on this journey. But sometimes it's all that's needed to shift things in a positive direction.

By repeatedly attuning and attending to our emotional experience, we're engaging in a process that brick by brick is restructuring the very foundation upon which we operate. Each time we recognize when we've gotten activated, each time we stop, drop, and stay with our emotional experience and find our way through it, each time we reflect on our experience and make sense of it, each time we do the work to engage mindfully with our partners, we are training our brain to work differently. We are strengthening new neural pathways that support our health. We are growing our capacity to be emotionally mindful.

That's the way forward.

CHAPTER TAKEAWAYS

- The core of our work is to free ourselves from a fear that is no longer warranted and reclaim our innate emotional capabilities so that we can have better relationships.

- While the four steps are arranged in a sequence that is designed to guide us through triggered moments in our lives, they also can be applied individually as needed.

- When we open ourselves up to greater intimacy, it's not uncommon to experience some anxiety afterward. Anticipating such an occurrence can help us to navigate it without being thrown.

- To have a secure relationship, we need to be able both to allow others to be close to us and assert our boundaries in a healthy way when needed.

- Defensive behaviors not only prevent the healthy expression of our feelings, needs, and desires but also thwart our ability to take in the good that comes our way.

- When we do the work to attend to the underlying forces that can unconsciously control our behavior, we free ourselves to have new experiences.

- By repeatedly attuning and attending to our emotional experience, we're engaging in a process that changes the way our brains work.

Becoming Real

"Once you are real you can't become unreal again.
It lasts for always."

MARGERY WILLIAMS BIANCO
The Velveteen Rabbit

Troy wiped the tears from his cheeks as he watched Andre drive away. They had had such a nice weekend together, and as he expected it was hard to say goodbye. *It always is,* Troy thought to himself. For both of them. Yet here they were, halfway through Troy's fellowship, living apart for the time being and managing to do okay. Well, more than okay. Things were really good between them. Despite the distance and all the back-and-forth trips, Troy felt more secure in his relationship with Andre than he'd ever felt with a partner.

Troy knew why. It wasn't a mystery. It was all the emotional work he had done. All the work he was doing. By finding the courage to be his true self with Andre, repeatedly taking the risk to share his feelings and to show up wholeheartedly, everything had changed. Troy felt as if he had stepped through a wall of fear and arrived more solidly in the world a whole person, able to be present in a way that heretofore had eluded him. Able to be completely himself. Able to show up and be real.

It wasn't always easy. In fact, sometimes it was pretty challenging. Sometimes Troy's emotions felt intense and were hard to stay with. Sometimes his anxiety would get the best of him. But each time Troy leaned in, each time he pushed himself to stay open and go the distance with Andre, he felt more confident in himself and more able to manage whatever might arise between them. He felt closer to Andre and more certain of their love for each other. Their connection felt solid. Their relationship real.

Troy thought about how different his experiences were in his past relationships. It was as if he'd been wearing lenses that made so many things seem scary and foreboding. Any bump in the road he encountered with a partner felt extreme and cause for alarm. But the more he was able to face his fear and move through it, the more his anxiety quieted down, and his vision cleared. Life came into sharper focus.

He could see himself more clearly. No longer trapped but with options. No longer possibly not good enough but someone worthy of love. And he could see Andre more objectively as well. No longer as a tyrant or saint but as a three-dimensional human being. Someone with his own history, his own fears, and his own struggles. Someone also just trying his best to make their relationship work. It was all such a relief.

Troy smiled as he recalled what it was like when Andre first got into town a few days ago. Andre had come directly from the airport to pick Troy up at work. Troy was waiting in the lobby when he arrived, and as they approached each other he noticed that Andre hesitated for a moment. Troy could tell Andre felt anxious and unsure of how he should greet him in this professional setting. *Should I give him a hug? Shake his hand? What would be appropriate here?* In the past, Troy might have not noticed Andre's self-consciousness. He might not have seen his vulnerability. Instead, he would have been caught up in his own emotional reaction. He would have seen Andre hesitate and thought that it was all about him. That he'd done something wrong. Or he'd worry that Andre was having second thoughts.

This time was different. Troy saw Andre's struggle, and it touched him. He found it endearing and felt his heart swell with love.

Troy stepped forward, put his arms around Andre, and hugged him. It felt so good to be together. *He's such a sweet man*, Troy thought to himself. *I'm so lucky.*

o   o   o

When we face our fears, when we lean in and share more of ourselves with our partners, when we explore new ways of being with them, everything changes. We loosen the grip of our early programming, and our range of options widens. Our perspective broadens, and our vision clears. We're able to see and experience ourselves, our partners, and our relationships in a more nuanced way. We're able to inhabit each moment more fully. We're able to respond more sensitively and skillfully. Our experiences become richer. Our relationships grow stronger. Our love deepens.

Relationships provide us with countless opportunities for growth and healing. Each challenge we face, each impasse we encounter holds the promise of something better. Each time we're triggered is an opportunity to break free from the past and realize our true potential, update our wiring, and strengthen our connections.

When we're mindful, we can see the path toward freedom. We can slow things down. We can stretch the space between stimulus and response and make a choice more aligned with our greater good.

So when the moment arrives, we can ask ourselves how we want to show up. Who do we want to be? What would be the best thing for our relationships? What would make them more secure?

And then we can lean in and do the work. We can bring forth the qualities in ourselves that will make the difference. That will fortify our connections. That will bring us closer. We can take a risk and share the feelings, needs, and desires we've been too afraid to share.

Whether we take a small step or go a lot further, it doesn't matter. Everything counts. It is a lifelong process that adds up over time. Each mindful effort we make grows our capacity to be present, to be real, to be connected.

We need to be patient and kind with ourselves as we do the work. We need to encourage and support ourselves as we peel away the layers and come more fully into the present moment. We need to remind ourselves of the importance of what we're doing. We need to remind ourselves of the reason for our efforts.

Doing the work to show up wholeheartedly in our relationships is an act of love. Love for ourselves and love for others. We're honoring our feelings and giving ourselves a chance to come into our own, to actualize. We're honoring our partners. We're showing them how much they mean to us. How much our relationship means to us. We're giving them all we've got. We're loving like we mean it.

Emotional mindfulness illuminates the path forward. Now you have the tools to guide you on your journey. May they serve you well. May they bring you all the riches that loving deeply can bring.

APPENDIX

Seeking Professional Help

At some point, you may want to work with a trained professional to help facilitate your emotional growth and healing. A therapist can help you increase your awareness and capacity to constructively experience your feelings, work through unresolved issues from the past, and overcome barriers that may be preventing you from being more emotionally present in your relationship. In addition, a couples therapist can help you and your partner get unstuck, develop healthy patterns of relating, and connect more deeply.

When seeking assistance for these matters, it's important to find a therapist who works *experientially*, which means that they practice a model of therapy that focuses on one's here and now emotional experience. As you know change happens through *experience* versus simply talking about it. Do some research, get referrals from trusted others who have had a positive experience in therapy, interview therapists over the phone, ask them about their approach, what kind of training they've completed, and how long they've been practicing. When you find a therapist who seems to fit the bill, have an initial consultation and see how it feels to you. It's essential that you work with someone with whom you feel understood, connected, safe, and confident in their ability to help you. You should be able to get a good sense of whether they're the right person to help you and if you're making progress fairly readily.

There are a number of different therapeutic approaches that emphasize emotional experience as a means to heal and change. AEDP, the model I practice, is particularly effective at working through attachment-related issues and helping people develop new, healthier ways of relating. Below you'll find a list of the experiential therapies I'm most familiar with and their respective websites, where you can learn more about them and search for a therapist in your area. In addition, you can find therapists through national and local professional association directories. Many states and provinces have more localized therapist directories that might be helpful in your search.

- Accelerated Experiential Dynamic Psychotherapy (AEDP) aedpinstitute.org

- Affect Phobia Therapy (APT): affectphobiatherapy.com

- Emotion(ally) Focused Therapy (EFT): iceeft.com and iseft.org

- Experiential Dynamic Therapy: iedta.com

- Eye Movement Desensitization and Reprocessing (EMDR): iedta.com

- Internal Family Systems (IFS): selfleadership.org

- Sensorimotor Psychotherapy: sensorimotorpsychotherapy. org

- Somatic Experiencing (SE): traumahealing.org

ACKNOWLEDGMENTS

"I can no other answer make,
but, thanks, and thanks."
WILLIAM SHAKESPEARE

As I think about all the people who in their own ways have helped make this book a reality, I feel so incredibly moved and blessed. It is with a heart full of gratitude that I thank:

Thomas Flannery, my literary agent, for finding the perfect home for this project.

Valerie Killeen, my editor at Central Recovery Press, for giving this book wings, and for the rest of the terrific team at CRP for their talent, care, hard work, and enthusiasm.

Jackie Frederick-Berner, my writing coach and trusted companion, for her literary wizardry and for helping me to write like I mean it (and then some).

My esteemed and cherished colleagues, Timothy Beyer, Diana Fosha, Linda Graham, and SueAnne Piliero, for their invaluable feedback on the manuscript, their generosity, and loving support.

The many teachers, colleagues, and scholars whose books surrounded me while I wrote and whose teachings were a constant source of inspiration, guidance, and support, most of whom are cited in the text.

Diana Fosha, the developer of AEDP, whose profound influence on my life and work is woven into every chapter of this book.

My students, supervisees, and trainees, for enlivening me with their desire to learn and challenging me to put my thinking into words.

My clients, past and present, for allowing me to be a part of their journeys, sharing their most vulnerable selves, and inspiring me to show up wholeheartedly.

My friends for being there at just the right times and for making me laugh.

My family, for their steadfast belief in me and for a love like no other.

And finally, my husband, Tim Beyer, for holding my hand (literally and figuratively) every step of the way and for providing me with the transformative experience of loving and being loved from which I write.

ABOUT THE AUTHOR

Ronald J. Frederick, PhD, is a clinical psychologist whose career has focused on the transforming power of emotional and relational experience. He is the author of the award-winning book *Living Like You Mean It: Use the Wisdom and Power of Your Emotions to Get the Life You Really Want* (Jossey-Bass, 2009), a senior faculty member of the Accelerated Experiential Dynamic Psychotherapy (AEDP) Institute, and Co-founder of the Center for Courageous Living in Beverly Hills, California. Noted for his warmth, humor, and engaging presentation style, Dr. Frederick lectures and facilitates workshops internationally.

REFERENCES

Introduction

1   National Opinion Research Council, *General Social Survey: Trends in Psychological Well-Being, 1972–2014* (Chicago, IL: University of Chicago Press, 2015).

2   Robert Johansson, et al., "Internet-Based Affect-Focused Psychodynamic Therapy for Social Anxiety Disorder: A Randomized Controlled Trial With 2-Year Follow-Up," *Psychotherapy*, Vol. 54, No. 4 (2017): 351–60.

3   John M. Gottman, *The Seven Principles for Making Marriage Work*, (New York, NY: Harmony Books, 2015).

4   Paul Gilbert, *The Compassionate Mind: A New Approach to Life's Challenges*, (Oakland, CA: New Harbinger Publications, 2009).

5   Christopher K. Germer, *The Mindful Path to Self-Compassion: Freeing Yourself from Destructive Thoughts and Emotions*, (New York, NY: Guilford Press, 2009).

6   Diana Fosha, *The Transforming Power of Affect*, (New York, NY: Basic Books, 2000).

Chapter One

1   John Bowlby, *Attachment: Attachment and Loss, Volume One* (New York, NY: Basic Books, 1969).

2   M.A. Bracket, et al., "Emotional intelligence: Implications for personal, social, academic, and workplace success," *Social and Personality Psychology Compass,* Vol. 5, No. 1 (2011): 88–103.

3   Adapted from Donald O. Hebb, *The Organization of Behavior* (New York, NY: John Wiley and Sons, Inc., 1949).

4   John Bowlby, *Loss: Sadness, and Depression, Volume 3* (New York, NY: Basic Books, 1980).

5   Joseph LeDoux, *Anxious: Using the Brain to Understand and Treat Fear and Anxiety* (New York, NY: Penguin Books, 2015).

Chapter Two

1   K. A. Brennan, C. L. Clark, and P. R Shaver, "Self-Report Measurement of Adult Romantic Attachment: An Integrative Overview," in *Attachment Theory and Close Relationships,* eds. J. A. Simpson and W. S. Rholes (New York, NY: Guilford Press,1998), 46–76.

2   Louis Cozolino, *The Neuroscience of Human Relationships* (New York, NY: W.W. Norton and Company, 2014).

3   Diana Fosha, *The Transforming Power of Affect* (New York, NY: The Perseus Book Group, 2000).

4   Daniel J. Siegel, *Mindsight: The New Science of Personal Transformation* (New York, NY: Bantam, 2010).

Chapter Three

1   Leigh McCullough, *Changing Character: Short Term Anxiety-Regulating Psychotherapy* (New York, NY: Basic Books, 1997).

2   Ronald J. Frederick, *Living Like You Mean It: Use the Wisdom and Power of Your Emotions to Get the Life You Really Want,* (San Francisco, CA: Jossey Bass, 2009).

3   Daphne M. Davis and Jeffrey A. Hayes, "What Are the Benefits of Mindfulness? A Practice Review of Psychotherapy-Related Research," *Psychotherapy*, Vol. 48, No. 2 (2012).

4   Jon Kabat-Zinn, *Wherever You Go There You Are: Mindfulness Meditation in Everyday Life*, (New York, NY: Hyperion,1994).

5   Jeffrey M. Schwartz and Rebecca Gladding, MD, *You Are Not Your Brain: The 4-Step Solution for Changing Bad Habits, Ending Unhealthy Thinking, and Taking Control of Your Life* (New York, NY: Avery Publishing, 2012).

6   Rick Hanson, *Buddha's Brain: The Practical Neuroscience of Happiness, Love, and Wisdom* (Oakland, CA: New Harbinger Publications, 2009).

7   Kristin Neff, *Self-Compassion: Stop Beating Yourself Up and Leave Insecurity Behind*, (New York, NY: Harper Collins, 2011).

8   Paul Gilbert, PhD., "The Practice of Learning and Change." Speech at Mindfulness and Compassion: The Art and Science of Contemplative Practice Conference. (Berkeley, CA: University of California Greater Good Science Center, 2015).

9   Matthew D. Lieberman, Naomi I. Eisenberger, Molly J. Crockett, et al, "Putting Feelings Into Words: Affect Labeling Disrupts Amygdala Activity in Response to Affective Stimuli," *Psychological Science*, Vol. 18, No. 5 (2007): 421–28.

10   If you'd like to learn more about the Triangle and our emotional dynamics, I invite you to check out my first book, *Living Like You Mean It: Use the Wisdom and Power of Your Emotions to Get the Life You Really Want.*

11   Diana Fosha, *The Transforming Power of Affect* (New York, NY: The Perseus Book Group, 2000).

12   Siegel, *Mindsight.*

13   Neff, *Self-Compassion.*

Chapter Four

1   "Stop and Drop" is a phrase I learned from my colleague SueAnne Piliero, PhD, to which I added "stay."

2   Daniel J. Siegel, *The Developing Mind: How Relationships and the Brain Interact to Shape Who We Are* (New York, NY: Guilford Press. 1999).

3   Pema Chödrön, *Taking the Leap: Freeing Ourselves from Old Habits and Fears* (Boulder, CO: Shambhala, 2009).

4   Daniel Goleman and Richard J. Davidson, *Altered Traits: Science Reveals How Meditation Changes Your Mind, Brain, And Body,* (New York, NY: Penguin Books 2017).

5   Joseph LeDoux, Anxious: *Using the Brain to Understand and Treat Fear and Anxiety* (New York, NY: Penguin Books 2016).

6   Richard Brown, MD and Patricia Gerbarg, MD, *The Healing Power of the Breath: Simple Techniques to Reduce Stress and Anxiety, Enhance Concentration, and Balance Your Emotions,* (Boulder, CO: Shambhala, 2012).

7   Sue Johnson, *Hold Me Tight: Seven Conversations for a Lifetime of Love,* (New York, NY: Little, Brown, 2008).

8   Richard Schwartz, *You Are the One You've Been Waiting For: Bringing Courageous Love to Intimate Relationships,* (Oak Park, IL: Trailheads Publications, 2008).

9   Giacomo Rizzolatti and Corrado Sinigaglia, *Mirrors in the Brain: How Our Minds Share Actions, Emotions, and Experience* (Oxford, UK: Oxford University Press, 2008).

Chapter Five

1   Diana Fosha, "Emotion and Recognition at Work: Energy, Vitality, Pleasure, Truth, Desire, and the Emergent Phenomenology of Transformational Experience," in *The Healing Power of Emotion: Affective Neuroscience, Development and Clinical Practice,* eds., Diana Fosha, PhD., Daniel J. Siegel, MD, and Marion Solomon, PhD (New York, NY: W.W. Norton & Company, 2009).

2   Diana Fosha, "Emotion, True Self, True Other, Core State: Toward a Clinical Theory of Affective Change Process," *Psychoanalytic Review*. Vol. 92, No. 4 (2005): 513–52.

3   Rick Hanson and Forrest Hanson, *Resilient: How to Grow an Unshakable Core of Calm, Strength, and Happiness* (New York, NY: Harmony Books, 2018).

4   Fosha, *The Healing Power of Emotion*.

5   Ibid.

6   Mark Epstein, *The Trauma of Everyday Life*, (New York, NY: Penguin Books, 2013).

7   James W. Pennebaker and Joshua M. Smyth. *Opening Up by Writing It Down: How Expressive Writing Improves Health and Eases Emotional Pain* (New York, NY: Guilford Press, 2016).

8   Daniel Goleman, *Emotional Intelligence: Why It Can Matter More Than IQ*, (New York, NY: Bantam Books, 1995).

9   Adapted from Sarah Thompson, *Focus on Emotions*, SA-exchange. February 9, 2017. https://sa-exchange.ca/ryersonsa-has-the-feels-201-part-1/.

10   Sue Johnson, *Love Sense: The Revolutionary New Science of Romantic Relationships*, (New York, NY: Little, Brown, 2013).

11   Eugene T. Gendlin, *Focusing-Oriented Psychotherapy: A Manual of the Experiential Method* (New York, NY: Guilford Press, 1996).

12   Diana Fosha, "Emotion, True Self, True Other, Core State: Toward a Clinical Theory of Affective Change Process," *Psychoanalytic Review*. Vol. 92, No. 4 (2005): 513–52.

13   Steven C. Hayes, Kirk D. Strosahl, and Kelly G. Wilson, *Acceptance and Commitment Therapy, Second Edition: The Process and Practice of Mindful Change,* (New York, NY: Guilford Press, 2016).

14   Adapted, in part, from Russ Harris, *The Happiness Trap: How to Stop Struggling and Start Living,* (Boston, MA: Shambhala/Trumpeter Books, 2008).

Chapter Six

1   Sharon Salzberg, *Real Love: The Art of Mindful Connection,* (New York, NY: Flatiron Books, 2017).

2   Brené Brown, *Daring Greatly: How the Courage to Be Vulnerable Transforms the Way We Live, Love, Parent, and Lead,* (New York: NY, Avery, 2015).

3   Linda Graham, *Bouncing Back: Rewiring Your Brain for Maximum Resilience and Well-Being,* (Novato, CA: New World Library, 2013).

4   John M. Gottman, and Nan Silver, *The Seven Principles for Making Marriage Work,* (New York, NY: Harmony Books, 2015).

5   Daniel Goleman, *Focus: The Hidden Driver of Excellence,* (New York, NY: HarperCollins, 2013).

6   Emily Esfahani Smith, "Masters of Love," *Atlantic,* June 12, 2014.

7   Pascal Vrtička, Frédéric Andersson, Didier Grandjean, David Sander, Patrik Vuilleumier, "Individual attachment style modulates human amygdala and striatum activation during social appraisal," (PLoS ONE 3(8): e2868, https://doi.org/10.1371/journal.pone.0002868, 2008).

8   Shunryu Suzuki and David Chadwick, *Zen Mind, Beginner's Mind: Informal Talks on Zen Meditation and Practice,* (Boston, MA: Shambhala Publications, 2011).

9   Daniel J. Siegel, *Mindsight: The New Science of Personal Transformation,* (New York, NY: Bantam Books, 2010).

10   Louis Cozolino, *Why Therapy Works: Using Our Minds to Change Our Brains* (New York, NY: W.W. Norton and Company, Inc., 2016).

11   Graham, *Bouncing Back.*

12   Daniel H. Lee and A.K. Anderson, "Reading What the Mind Thinks from How the Eye Sees," *Psychological Science,* Vol. 28, No. 4 (2017): 494–503.

13   Susan Gillis Chapman, *The Five Keys to Mindful Communication: Using Deep Listening and Mindful Speech to Strengthen Relationships, Heal Conflicts and Accomplish Your Goals,* (Boston, MA: Shambhala Publications 2012).

14   Germer, *The Mindful Path to Self-Compassion..*

15   Fosha, *The Transforming Power of Affect.*

16   Pat Ogden, PhD and Janina Fisher, *Sensorimotor Psychotherapy: Interventions for Trauma and Attachment,* (New York, NY: W.W. Norton and Company, 2015).

17   Brené Brown, *The Gifts of Imperfection: Let Go of Who You Think You're Supposed to Be and Embrace Who You Are,* (Centre City, MN: Hazelden Publishing, 2010).